To Be One with God

*Seven Journeys to
the Meaning of Life*

SHAFEEN ALI

DEDICATION

To My Beloved Spiritual Father,
the Spirit of my life,
To My Loving Wife Iram,
the Pillar of my life,
To My Nurturing Parents Sherali and Zubeda,
the Teachers of my life,
To My Caring Daughters Isra and Saira,
the Keepers of my life,
To All My Beloved Spiritual Brothers and Sisters,
the Purpose of my life.

ACKNOWLEDGMENTS

This book wouldn't be possible without the support of family and friends who have been there for me, encouraging me to trust my Inner Imam and to fulfill his vision. I would particularly like to acknowledge the following:

1. Zehra and Shehzad, my siblings, for always seeing the best in me and trusting my ability to write and publish this book.

2. Aslam and Shanaz, my parents-in-law, for their continuous support and unending prayers for our family.

3. Faizan, Sanya, Sohail, and Kiran, my siblings-in-law, for opening up their homes and hearts to support this very important project of my life.

4. Shaila (myhouseofdesign.com), for designing this book's beautiful cover and for mentoring me on the writing and publishing process.

5. Rozi (scholastic.sessions@gmail.com) and Sonia, for their immense effort in meticulously editing the book and encouraging me to believe in myself and this project.

6. Ryan (buildmyidea.org), for helping me to articulate my Inner Imam and coaching me to build my idea and turn it into reality.

7. Perwaiz, for being a ray of light and loving acceptance in the times I doubted myself the most.

8. Azmina Suleman, for her beautiful book *A Passage to Eternity*. As a fellow Shia Ismaili Muslim, her decision to publish her atypical experience and understanding of eternal truths, gave me the courage to do the same.

9. Joanna Penn (thecreativepenn.com), for her amazing blogs and courses on what it takes to publish a book.

10. Dr. Wayne Dyer (drwaynedyer.com), for teaching me not to die with my music still in me and for inspiring me at the "Writing from Your Soul" writer's workshop. Dr. Dyer, you are still alive inspiring me in my heart.

CONTENTS

WHY THIS BOOK?

What is the meaning of my life? In every age and time, mankind asks this question. Scholars, philosophers, and seekers respond with answers. This book is my attempt. My answer is that the meaning of life is to be one with God. Other questions that follow are, "What does it mean to be one with God?" and "How does one embark on such a journey?" In this book, I explore seven journeys to be one with God. Each journey represents a path to come closer and closer to the spirit that created the universe. These journeys have unfolded in my life, within my heart. Through this book, I aspire to share these journeys with you.

Every piece of art unfolds on a canvas, a background upon which it's drawn or painted. This book has unfolded upon my inner being. Ever since I was young, I have conversed with my inner being: a friend, who resides within, always there, especially in times of difficulty. Today, this friend is my constant companion. I consult him in the smallest of matters. I call him my "Inner Imam." In Arabic, the word "Imam" means "one who leads the way." He leads the way of my life and directs me like a compass to where I must go in every moment. For me, he's the stuff that life is made of: the spirit, the breath, the light, the love, that permeates every aspect of being and living, for my life, for all life. For me, he's God.

What is God? God is a word, a word that holds a unique meaning for each and every one of us. This word strives to capture the knowledge and experience of a higher reality beyond our physical lives. Since each of us experiences his/her physical life personally, each conceives of this higher reality uniquely. It's as if four blind people are asked to describe an elephant by touching it. The first touches the trunk and thinks the elephant to be like a water pipe. The second touches the ear and thinks the elephant to be like a fan. The third touches the leg and thinks the elephant to be like a pillar. The fourth touches the back and thinks the elephant to be like a throne.[1] None of the men conceive of the elephant as a whole. They only know what they know depending on where they reside in relation to the elephant. It's the same of God. We often describe God as an absolute reality that's the same for all of us. In experience, however, each and every one of us conceives of God in a personal way to fulfill his/her own meaning of life.

The God that I share in this book is my experience of my Inner Imam. He's my Spiritual Father, the one in whose being, in whose spirit, I originated, and so did all of life. Before I came into existence, I lived and breathed in his essence as his essence. One day, he sent me forth from his being to experience life. Now, I am in physical life, striving to return back to him, to be one with him, to be one with God. All of life reflects his essential being. It reflects a small piece of his grandness like the trunk, the leg, the ear, or the back of the elephant. In order to realize him, I have two options. The first is to explore him externally from every perspective like the blind men looking for clues. The second is to dive into the part of him within me, my Inner Imam, and to live out the whole through the part. I have taken the second approach and embodied it in this book.

It's as if there's a grand ocean and there's a droplet from that ocean. Though the droplet is small in size compared to the ocean, the chemical foundation of the droplet is the same as the ocean—H_2O. If the droplet tries to understand the ocean by traveling it in its entirety, it will be an impossible task, for the ocean never sits still, always moving and expanding. But if the droplet understands its own essential nature as H_2O, it will truly understand the nature of the entire ocean from its part; hence, it will see the whole as a grander projection of itself on the screen of life. With this book, I share the part of me which reflects the

---

[1] Jalalu·'d-din Rumi, "The Elephant in a Dark Room," in *The Masnavi I Ma'navi of Rumi*, trans. Edward Whinfield (London, UK: Forgotten Books, 2008), 107-108.

whole. I share the essential nature in me that projects the essential nature of God.

It's my aspiration that as you read this book, you'll find your relationship with God and where you would like to go forward with that relationship. I have shared with you seven journeys that have been active in my life to be one with him. I have tried to conceive of these journeys through your life as well as mine. In each journey, you'll hear directly from God as well as teachers who we believe achieved oneness with him. Some of you may perceive this as my imagination. Some of you may perceive this as my spiritual experiences that I'm sharing with you. In the end, my objective is for you to experience God as I experience him.

What's the utility of sharing my experience with you? If each of us conceives of God in his/her own way, why not let each be on his/her own? I believe we are each a reflection of God's essence, of his love and light, intended to brighten up each other's life. We learn from each other in all aspects of life. Each of us has his/her own tastes of what he/she likes to eat and yet we appreciate each other's opinions of what's good at which restaurant. The same is true today of all sorts of things from entertainment to contractors we would hire to upgrade our homes. If this is true for all other aspects of life, shouldn't it also be true for our search for God and how we strive to be one with him? If the search for God is the ultimate meaning of life, shouldn't we all be writing a book or a blog to tell others how we are personally and communally experiencing God in our lives?

I have observed that God has become a mystery today and either he's collecting dust inside books or is debated and discussed in philosophy classes. Our secularized culture has limited God to a private practice rather than a public truth; accordingly, those who have had a personal experience of God are choosing to remain silent so that they may not interfere with someone else's perception or understanding of him. This is contradictory to my experience of God for I live, breath and have my being in God. How can you separate God from my life without also separating me from myself?

While growing up in this context, I have tried to preserve my faith and life in God. While being respectful to give others the space to find their own way of connecting with the divine, I have felt encouraged and empowered to express my own faith, its love and light. Many who have come into contact with me in the corporate world have seen God's light in my being. They have appreciated that presence in my work. This book is my attempt to take that further by unveiling what lives in my mind, heart and soul. My hope is to inspire a culture in which each of us is proud of his/her personal relationship with God while open to the diverse ways others may personalize this relationship.

As you embark on these journeys to find the meaning of life, to be one with God, you'll observe that this is a two way journey. It's not just us who as human beings are reaching out for God to be one with him. He's also reaching out to be one with us. In its innermost sense, I believe this book to be God's attempt to reach out to me, and through me, to reach out to each and every one of you. I have often been a mere spectator witnessing his spirit write this book. I can relate with the words of Jesus when he explained to his audience, "The words that I say to you I do not speak on my own; but the Father who dwells in me does his works."[2] As I have felt my faith and soul expand through this book, I hope you too experience the same. As I have witnessed him make himself known in my life and in all life through this book, I hope you too realize the same.

Some of you may be wondering how my personal religious outlook aligns with this book. I am a Shia Ismaili Muslim. All Muslims believe in the oneness of God and in Prophet Muhammad (peace be upon him) as the final Prophet of God. All Shia Muslims believe that after the Prophet's death, spiritual interpretation of God's final message and guidance to humanity

---

[2] John 14:10 (NRSV).

continued through the Institution of Imamat, established as per divine designation and initiation through the Prophet. All Shia Ismaili Muslims believe that the divinely designated Imam, today, is His Highness the Aga Khan, Shah Karim Al-Hussaini. He's the forty-ninth hereditary Imam and a direct descendant of the Prophet through his cousin and son-in-law, Ali, the first Imam, and his wife Fatima, the Prophet's daughter.

As a Shia Ismaili Muslim, my complete loyalty, devotion, and obedience are to the Imam of the Time. For those who give their allegiance to him, the Imam of the Time is the source of direction and progress in both spiritual and material matters. Therefore, there may be a question in some minds as to how the guidance of this "Inner Imam" can be followed when there's a physical Imam present to guide us.

The answer for me lies in the essential nature of the religion of Islam. As His Highness the Aga Khan has often stated, in Islam, there's no dichotomy between the spiritual and the physical realms - between *din* and *duniya* - as they are referred to in the Arabic vernacular. They are intertwined.[3] Consequently, in the practice of my faith, there's no dichotomy between the spiritual, personal, inner Imam and the physical, communal, outer Imam. I believe that the spirit of God that lives and guides in my inner, spiritual Imam is the same spirit of God that lives and guides in the outer, physical Imam. The outer is a reminder of the inner, the physical a gateway to the spiritual.

Moreover, you'll find in this book many examples of how my religion, and the community that espouses it, have helped me

---

[3] "Riad Naguib El-Rais Interview, 'The Critical Time' (Al Mustaqbal, Cairo, Egypt)," Nanowisdoms.org, December 20, 1986, accessed November 23, 2015, http://www.nanowisdoms.org/nwblog/2074/; and "Address by His Highness the Aga Khan to the Tutzing Evangelical Academy Upon Receiving the 'Tolerance' Award (Tutzing, Germany)," AKDN.org, May 20, 2006, accessed November 23, 2015, http://www.akdn.org/speech/605/Tolerance-Award-from-the-Evangelical-Academy-of-Tutzing.

experience oneness with God. My intention is not to proselytize or advocate that the reader convert to my religion. Instead, my intention is to demonstrate through my example that religion <u>can</u> be a gateway to spiritual truths just as spiritual truths <u>can</u> enrich and enhance one's experience of religion. The word "religion" comes from the Latin root *religare* which means "to bind." The word "spirituality" comes from the Latin root *spiritus* which means "the breath." Together, religion and spirituality serve a united purpose: to bind the individual to the spirit or the breath of God within him which is his essence.

Please note: **This book is not intended in anyway to be the official voice of the religion of Islam or Shia Islam or Shia Ismaili Islam. Everything that's said is personal and not communal.** I'm not writing this book to articulate my religious community's outlook on oneness with God. Rather, this book is **my own personal endeavor** to realize and express the voice of the divine within me. That voice sees all as one and one as all. It speaks from a place in which all diversity collapses into a unity, in which all faiths are one, all people are one, and all life is one.

I wish you wonderful journeys up ahead as you venture deeper into this book and unveil the mystery of my life, of your life, of all life. I humbly believe that God is waiting for you on the other side. He has been waiting eternally for this moment for you to look deeper into his mind, his heart, his soul and find your own mind, your own heart, your own soul.

Safe travels fellow seeker. May you find God in your life in every breath that you take and may he breathe his life in every moment you are awake!

BEFORE WE BEGIN

When I often think of a journey to be one with God, I think of a bird that yearns to be one with the sky. The bird flies and flies and tries its best to reach the sky. The sky, of course, is infinite space, hence, unreachable. It's the background upon which all of life takes place. But the bird is determined and struggles with all its strength and courage to reach the sky. There comes a point when the bird, completely exhausted from the flight, starts falling to the ground. On seeing the bird in such a state, the sky lowers itself and uplifts the bird making the bird one with it. The bird becomes the sky and the sky becomes the bird. In a sublime state of being, the bird experiences and re-experiences itself to be the ultimate. In that same moment, the ultimate completely reveals itself through the bird. There's still some emptiness left in the being of the bird that the sky fills in with its essence. Finally, the bird is ready to go back taking the memory and experience of the sky back to the earth.

The journeys to be one with God in this book follow the same pattern. It's man who ASPIRES to be one with God, and PREPARES to be one with him. But ultimately, it's through God that man ARRIVES at oneness with him. Consequently, man EXPERIENCES that oneness as God operating in man and man operating in God. The experience is so grand that man RELIVES it in order to capture its beauty and bliss. Now, man has many questions and he CONVERSES with God to find the remaining answers, to fill the remaining holes in his knowledge and experience. Finally, man REALIZES his oneness with God after reflection on the entire journey, on what has ultimately changed in his being. He takes a renewed sense of himself back to his life and lives that life in harmony with God.

Each of the seven journeys is organized in the stages capitalized above. These stages are unique not just in their content but also in the voice representing that content. They

7

are explained in more detail as follows:

STAGE 1: ASPIRE

This stage is the general overview for the specific journey. It's presented through my voice, SHAFEEN, as I describe the journey through teachings given to us by God and through the example of his teachers across time and age. In this stage, we develop our aspirations to be one with God by understanding what the journey entails. If we are going on a physical trip, the ASPIRE stage would include desiring to take the trip, researching the attractions and the activities, and finalizing the commitment to travel.

STAGE 2: PREPARE

This stage is the inner work one undertakes to prepare for the journey. It's presented through the voice of MAN, representing one of us, as he struggles with all that holds him back from embarking on this journey, and then overcomes it. There's always a story in the middle of this stage that marks the turning point for that individual. In this stage, with this individual, we, too, struggle through the darkness that prevents many of us from making the journey to God and find the light that allows us to take off. If we are going on a physical trip, the PREPARE stage would include clearing the barriers to taking the trip, then packing the bags and boarding the plane or the vehicle to take us abroad.

STAGE 3: ARRIVE

This stage is the knowledge and enlightenment we receive as we arrive at the destination of the journey. It's presented through the voice of GOD, providing the wisdom we need to be uplifted to his view of life. There's always a story at the beginning of this stage which God uses to center us on the essential teachings of the journey. In this stage, we are enriched and enveloped with God's love and light allowing us to partake in his essence. If we are going on a physical trip, the ARRIVE stage would include the plane or vehicle arriving at the trip location, and the receipt of the guidance we'll need for the mountains we'll climb, the holy places we'll visit, or the forests we'll explore.

STAGE 4: EXPERIENCE

This stage is the actual experience of oneness with God, the core experience of the journey. It's presented through the voice of a TEACHER of God, who has become one with him, and is having a man in God-God in man experience. In this stage, we participate in an event or a situation in the life of the teacher and live out that experience with him. If we are going on a physical trip, the EXPERIENCE stage would be the actual experience of climbing the mountains, visiting the holy places, or exploring the forest.

STAGE 5: RELIVE

This stage is the reliving of the experience of oneness with God from another point of view in the journey. It's presented through my voice, SHAFEEN, as I remember and relive experiences of oneness with God, in my own life. Often, when we look at the teachers of humanity, we regard them as inspirational, but their lives as far removed from our own. We are unable to relate with them since they lived in a different time and age. In this stage, we strive to relive the truths of this journey grounded in another life, my own, as lived in this time and age. This validates that the experience is possible for each and every one of us no matter the culture or society we live in. If we are going on a physical trip, the RELIVE stage would be an alternate experience of climbing the mountains, visiting the holy places, or exploring the forests, reliving and solidifying the lessons from the first.

STAGE 6: CONVERSE

This stage addresses the questions that we may still have after experiencing and reliving the journey. It's presented through the voice of MAN and GOD. In this stage, we witness a Q&A between Man and God as relevant to the journey. The questions are intended to clarify any missing pieces in our knowledge and experience of the journey. If we are going on a physical trip, the CONVERSE stage would be the additional questions that we would ask of our tour guide to get a more in-depth understanding and experience of the attractions and the activities.

STAGE 7: REALIZE

This is the final stage of the journey. It helps us reflect on the entire journey and how our being - and living - has changed forever. It's presented through your voice, the READER, as you review the summary of the journey and reflect on questions to assimilate this experience into your lives. In this stage, we look at the journey through real-eyes and prepare to return back to our day to day life with enlightened knowing and being. If we are going on a physical trip, the REALIZE stage would be the plane or vehicle ride back to our point of origination, with the opportunity to reflect upon and integrate into our lives the new growth and experiences.

At the beginning of the stages of each journey are inspirations that summarize that specific stage. In some cases, these inspirations take the form of instructions while in other cases they are affirmations. If we need a quick reminder of each journey as a whole, we only need to look at the inspiration for the ASPIRE portion of each journey, the stage intended as the overview of the journey. If we want a thorough understanding of each journey, all we need to do is to look at the seven inspirations that summarize the seven stages of each journey.

Though the journeys are organized in a sequence based on my personal preference, you may choose to experience them individually in your own way. For example, if you choose to start with the Journey of Union with God, you may do so and work your way backwards rather than forwards. You may also decide to read the journeys in the order that best corresponds to your interest in becoming one with God.

In order to help you choose, each of the seven journeys has been highlighted below in the order they are presented in this book. Along with the journey is included the respective inspiration from the ASPIRE stage which summarizes each journey. Moreover, God plays a specific role in each journey that has been clarified, through a phrase, associated with the acronym G.o.d. as indicated below.

Journey of Knowledge to God (Genesis of diversity)
Seek to know God in all of life.
Knowing God is the way to know yourself.

Journey of Purpose through God (Gate of destiny)
Hear God calling you to your true life purpose.
That purpose is why you exist.

Journey of Presence in God (Guru of detachment)
Let go of everything so that you can rest in God.
Resting in God is most productive.

Journey of Guidance from God (Giver of direction)
Turn within to hear the voice of God.
That voice knows and shows the way.

Journey of Giving of God (Garden of delight)
Give the best of yourself to all.
That good reflects God, in your life, in all life.

Journey of Love for God (Ground of devotion)
Love all ways to live in the heart of God.
God's heart loves all, friend and foe.

Journey of Union with God (Goal of devotee)
Remember God all the time to re-member yourself with God.
Then peace emanates through you and all of life partakes in it.

It's my hope and prayer that as you complete each journey, you feel closer and closer to the spirit of God within and without. It's also my hope and prayer that you find a deeper spiritual connection with other brothers and sisters in life regardless of their religious or spiritual affinity. I strongly believe that we can't give to others what we don't have within ourselves. I also believe that we can't give to ourselves what we don't have for others. Therefore, this book strives to have us see God in ourselves as well as in others.

Safe travels, fellow seeker. May your life be filled with God's light on each turn on every corner. May his life flow through your being in each moment in every manner!

Journey of Knowledge to God

God as the <u>G</u>enesis <u>of</u> <u>d</u>iversity

Beauty is life when life unveils her holy face.
But you are life and you are the veil.
Beauty is eternity gazing at itself in a mirror.
But you are eternity and you are the mirror.

— Khalil Gibran, *The Prophet*

JOURNEY OF KNOWLEDGE TO GOD
STAGE 1: ASPIRE

Seek to know God in all of life.
Knowing God is the way to know yourself.

Voice of Shafeen

Once, Mullah Nasruddin came charging down the bazaar on his donkey. His neighbors and friends had never seen him this anxious and worried. He was looking for something. One of his friends asked, "Mullah, what are you looking for?" Nasruddin answered: "My donkey. I remember seeing him before I left home today. When I returned home, he wasn't there. I have searched for him everywhere. Where could he be?" Before the friend could point out that Nasruddin was sitting on his donkey, Nasruddin charged into another direction, anxiously looking for the same donkey that he himself was riding.[4]

Many of us seek the phenomenon, the mystery that we call God. We may spend our entire lives resolving this mystery. Unable to prove that God exists, we may come to the conclusion that he's a myth, a concept that we have made up. In reality, just like Nasruddin's donkey, God is the mechanism, the faculty through which we search for God himself. We don't find him unless we first look within. It's only because God exists that we exist, that our search for him exists. He is the stuff that life is made up of, and so all thinking, seeking, pondering, reflecting, and discovering—all pursuit and achievement of knowledge—happens through and in God.

In this journey of "Knowledge to God," we strive to become one with God by knowing God within ourselves and within all

---

[4] Adapted from Anthony De Mello, S. J., "The Search for the Ass," in *The Song of the Bird*, 2nd ed. (Anand, India: Gujarat Sahitya Prakash, 1982), 11.

of life. In all pursuits of knowledge, the seeker goes after what he seeks. On this journey, we realize that the seeker and the "seeked" are one and the same. The difference between the two is superficial, caused by man's limitation to see the spirit that embodies all of life. Once man is able to see this spirit, all dichotomy collapses into an integrated unity, and all life becomes one. Accordingly, the best definition of God on this journey is GOD as the Genesis Of Diversity.

God is the genesis, the beginning of all that exists. In his creation, he has taken the form of everything, material and spiritual. Nothing can have its own life outside of God; thus, everything lives and breathes in God. All diversity that we see in life is caused by the spirit of God, the ultimate source and destination of all living and being. We witness this truth validated today, both by spiritual teaching, as well as scientific seeking.

Spiritual teachings across time and age have talked about the spirit of God as ever-present in our experience of life. God, speaking through Muhammad, says in the Qur'an: "To God belong the East and the West: whithersoever ye turn, there is the presence of God. For God is All-Pervading, All-Knowing."[5] It's not only the physical turning, the turning without, which is implied in this verse, it's also the spiritual turning, the turning within, which is inferred. This is clarified further in another verse in the Qur'an, which says: "We will soon show them Our signs in the Universe and **in their own souls**, until it will become quite clear to them that it is the truth."[6] God is promising mankind that he'll show them his truth, his existence, his kingdom, both outside as well as within themselves.

Six hundred years before Muhammad, another teacher Jesus,

---

[5] Qur'an 2:115 (Yusuf Ali). The Arabic term "Allah" was replaced with the English equivalent "God" in this quote as is the practice in certain contemporary translations of the Qur'an.

[6] Qur'an 41:53 (Shakir) [emphasis mine].

also provided insights to see God's truth. He summarized his primary reason for being sent by God to the people as the need "to proclaim the good news of the kingdom of God."[7] Many in Jesus' time associated the idea of a kingdom of God with a physical kingdom. They thought that God would create a new political rule through a Messiah. Jesus corrected this by explaining: "The kingdom of God cometh not with observation: Neither shall they say, Lo here! or, lo there! for, behold, the kingdom of God is within you."[8] Jesus emphasized the inner recognition of the kingdom of God, God's authority, his rule, in one's life. This was why he was sent: to help us cultivate that kingdom within, to find God living and breathing wherever we turn.

In the Old Testament, we hear God asking the rhetorical question: "Do I not fill the heavens and the earth?"[9] In the New Testament, we hear the answer to this question: "All things were made by Him, and without Him was not anything made that was made. In Him was life, and that life was the Light of men."[10] God is, therefore, the stuff that life is made up of. He is the cause and the effect of all of life: the essence that creates and sustains all of life and the light or the intelligence that guides mankind to this truth.

Thousands of years before Muhammad and Jesus Christ, another teacher, Krishna, speaking from God consciousness, validates the same truth. He says:

The brightness of the sun, which lights the world, the brightness of the moon and the fire – these are my glory. With a drop of my energy I enter the earth and support all

---

[7] Luke 4:43 (NIV).

[8] Luke 17:20-21 (KJV).

[9] Jeremiah 23:24 (NASB).

[10] John 1:3-4 (NIV).

TO BE ONE WITH GOD

creatures. Through the moon, the vessel of life-giving fluid, I nourish all plants. I enter breathing creatures and dwell within as the life-giving breath. I am the fire in the stomach which digests all food. Entering into every heart, I give the power to remember and understand; it is I again who take that power away. All the scriptures lead to me; I am their author and their wisdom.[11]

In alignment with spiritual teachings, scientific seeking has also led mankind to recognize a spirit behind all that occurs in the universe. Albert Einstein, one of the greatest scientists of the twentieth century, spoke to this spirit when he said: "Every one who is seriously engaged in the pursuit of science becomes convinced that the laws of nature manifest the existence of a spirit vastly superior to that of men, and one in the face of which we with our modest powers must feel humble."[12]

More recently, in her book, "The Field," investigative journalist Lynne Mctaggart has gathered scientific evidence for what she refers to as the "Zero Point Field." She discusses many scientific experiments that measure, analyze, and test psychic phenomena, energetic healings, remote intention, and coherence and communication between particles at the subatomic level. Mctaggart suggests that the "Zero Point Field" is a sea of energy which connects everything and forms the background, the foundation, for these anomalies to take place.[13] For her, this is evidence of the life force which some call collective consciousness or the Holy Spirit, what we have

---

[11] Eknath Easwaran, trans., *The Bhagavad Gita*, 2nd ed. (Tomales, CA: Nilgiri Press, 2007), 15:12-15.

[12] Max Jammer, *Einstein and Religion: Physics and Theology* (Princeton, NJ: Princeton University Press, 1999), 93.

[13] Lynne McTaggart, prologue to *The Field: The Quest for the Secret Force of the Universe* (New York, NY: HarperCollins Publishers, 2002), XVII.

referred to as the spirit of God.[14]

One way to substantiate this field is through a mysterious occurrence at the subatomic level which even Einstein couldn't explain. He called it, "spooky actions at a distance."[15] At the subatomic level, two particles may entangle in such a way that even if they are separated by hundreds or thousands of miles, they still continue to communicate and influence each other. When the state of one of these particles is changed, the other particle immediately adjusts its state, in response to the change in the original particle. From a traditional Newtonian scientific perspective, there's no reason why these particles should behave in such a manner. There's no visible or detectable connection between them. Yet, the change is so instantaneous that it's as if the news of the change travels faster than the speed of light (the fastest speed known to man).[16] There must be some field, some force, which we can't account for with our physical capacities, that communicates between these particles and impacts them. This is that "Zero Point Field," a spiritual field that originates and is sustained by the spirit of the divine.

We can all relate to "spooky actions at a distance" in our day-to-day lives. A loved one is driving, and his/her car breaks down on a road miles away, if not in another city or another country all together. Suddenly, we start getting the eerie feeling that something is wrong with our loved one. We pick up the phone and call him/her. He/she is surprised: "My car just broke down. How did you know that something was wrong?" We can't explain it but somehow we knew that our loved one

---

[14] McTaggart, prologue to *The Field*, XVIII.

[15] Bruce Rosenblum, interview by Thomas McFarlane, Holos Forum 4, no. 1 (2008), March 2007, accessed August 5, 2015, http://www.holosforum.org/v4n1/rosenblum.html.

[16] "Quantum Entanglement Simplified - Microscopic Universe," accessed November 23, 2015, https://www.youtube.com/watch?v=PWuCXcoXNts.

needed help. There's no material communication that lets us know this. But, there's a spiritual connection, knowledge transferred through a spiritual mechanism, an energy that underlies all of life.

Accordingly, both spiritual teachings as well as scientific seeking have validated the truth of the famous new age adage: "We are not human beings having a spiritual experience; we are spiritual beings having a human experience."[17] As spiritual beings, we are connected to each other and to all of life; hence, we are able to impact each other through exchange of inspiration and information. This explains many of the mysteries of our world today, from psychic phenomena, to spirit communication, to miraculous healings.

Knowing ourselves as spiritual beings and all of life as the spiritual essence of God has immense repercussions for how we live our lives. With this awareness, we are empowered to shape the circumstances of our lives rather than letting those circumstances overcome us. Life becomes a school. Each experience contributes to our knowledge and experience of our spirituality and hence God. We realize that when we hurt another, we hurt ourselves, for the other is from our own essence. The same becomes true if we help or benefit another. There are no enemies, for everyone is a reflection of God. There are no tragedies, for we understand the nature of the physical as temporal and the nature of the spiritual as eternal. Krishna teaches us:

> The body is mortal, but that which dwells in the body is immortal and immeasurable.... You were never born; you will never die. You have never changed; you can never change. Unborn, eternal, immutable, immemorial, you do not die when the body dies.[18]

---

[17] Robert J. Furey, *The Joy of Kindness* (Chestnut Ridge, NY: Crossroad Publishing Company, 1993), 138.

[18] Easwaran, *Gita*, 2:18-20.

The great spiritual teachers understood the ultimate nature of life as spirit, as nothing gained or lost, born or dead. Consequently, they were able to demonstrate great compassion and resilience in the face of extreme trials and tribulations. The Buddha advises his followers: "Though robbers who are highwaymen should cut you up in pieces limb by limb with a two-handed saw, yet if the mind of any one of you should take offense ..., such a one is no follower of my Teaching."[19]

In order for us to realize what the teachers knew, we must make God the only authority in our lives. We must become like little children, willing to trust the eternal parent to lead the way. This was taught by Jesus when he was asked by his disciples: "Who is the greatest in the kingdom of heaven?"[20] Jesus called a little child to him and said: "Truly I tell you, unless you change and become like little children, you will never enter the kingdom of heaven. Therefore, whoever takes the lowly position of this child is the greatest in the kingdom of heaven."[21]

As we, too, give ourselves into the hands of God, completely submitting to him, we allow him to lead us through his will to his knowledge and the knowledge of all of life in him. We see his spirit everywhere, and life becomes filled with his love and light. Thereafter, wherever we turn, there is the spirit of God, the kingdom of God, within and without.

---

[19] Robert A. Mitchell, *The Buddha: His Life Retold* (New York, NY: Paragon House, 1989), 141.

[20] Matthew 18:1 (ESV).

[21] Matthew 18:3-4 (NIV).

JOURNEY OF KNOWLEDGE TO GOD
STAGE 2: PREPARE

See yourself as inter-connected with all of life.
You are a part of the whole that is God.

Voice of Man

Dear God,

Where are you?

I have been looking for you for so long. I tire to see your face, to be in your kingdom, to know your truth. I have visited the mosques, the synagogues, the churches and the temples. In all these places, I couldn't locate you. Everywhere I see shrines venerating you but you are nowhere to be found. You are a mystery, a secret known by a few which has been forgotten or so well hidden that even the seekers know not the address. I see many today that call themselves your believers but live far from your truth. I see many others today that live by your truth but shy away from claiming themselves believers. All kinds of injustices happen today in your name. All kinds of good happen today in the name of man without any credit given to you. Where have we lost you? Where did we go wrong? What message did we forget to read or understand or implement or teach? What scripture is missing today that was sent by you but hidden under the rubble of ignorance, or even worse, intentionally buried under the weight of lies?

Dear God, I miss you so. I remember my parents telling me that whenever I face difficulties, to call upon you and you would come to my help and save me. But dear God, with which name should I call you? Some tell me to call upon "Jesus," others tell me to call upon "Yahweh," some call you "Allah," and others call you "Bhagvan." With which name do you like to be called? Man has separated you into separate homes, separate names, separate beliefs, and separate identities. Man has separated himself also into separate religions, separate races, separate cultures, and separate communities. They all claim you belong to them, you are only theirs, and that salvation is only through their way and no other way. Is this true? Are you only to be found in one place and not another? Do you only live in one heart and not another?

Dear God, when a man is in need of blood at a hospital, they don't need to know his name, religion, or creed to provide the right blood supply. They only need to know his blood type. I am in need of spiritual sustenance. So what's my spiritual blood type? What type of faith will pump new life into my spiritual heart? Please show me the way for I am truly one of the lost.

Dear God, I now sit in silence seeking your guidance … My heart stirs as I remember a story I had forgotten:

Once, Mullah Nasruddin visited a devout Muslim friend. The friend had a guest room with a bed facing the window. The window faced east, towards the holy city of Mecca, containing the house of God, the Kaaba. The friend advised: "Dear Nasruddin, make sure that you sleep with your head towards Mecca, out of respect for God." Nasruddin was an active sleeper and tossed and turned and ended up with his feet facing Mecca. When Nasruddin awoke, he found the friend staring down at him. The friend scolded Nasruddin: "You must not point your feet towards God! You must point your head towards God and your feet away from him!" Nasruddin convinced his friend that it wouldn't happen again but the same occurred for three consecutive mornings. On the third morning, seeing his friend bursting with anger, Nasruddin held out his feet and said: "Point my feet where God is not!"[22]

---

[22] Adapted from "Where is God Not," The Outrageous Wisdom of Nasruddin, accessed November 12, 2015, http://www.nasruddin.org/pages/stories/whereisGodnot.html.

Dear God, it was as if I was digging for treasure and this story struck gold, deep within my heart. I received the answers to all my questions. You aren't anywhere because you are everywhere. It's as if we are looking for air, and we don't see it anywhere because it's everywhere. From the sun in the sky that shines life into every living being to the blood that circulates life into our physical bodies, you are present, you are living. You have manifested your signs everywhere for us to see. Take a hummingbird, for example. This wondrous creature has a heart that beats more than 1,200 times per minute. It has wings that beat about 80 times per second.

Dear God, no matter how much knowledge we have acquired, we can't recreate a hummingbird the way you have created. In fact, we can't create anything mechanical that has the ability to think and do for itself as well as adapt. You, on the other hand, have created a universe filled with life which sustains itself and has done so for billions of years. Yet, some call this universe an accident, a mere coincidence. When we desire to cook an egg, a mind intends the cooking, a hand cracks the egg, an arm stirs and flips it, a nose smells the fragrance, and eyes observe the entire process making sure the egg doesn't burn. If so much intelligence and action is required to cook a simple egg, how much more would be required to create and then sustain this universe? How could we then believe all of this to be a mere coincidence?

Dear God, now I find the answers to my questions. I didn't see you in all the holy places because I was looking for a ONE separate from the WHOLE. Now I realize that all of life is wholly, including the holy places. I also realize that all the names that are used to call upon you point to the same essence. It doesn't really matter which name I use to connect with you. As long as the name resonates in my heart, your presence will be found. I see your presence in all of life, including my brothers and sisters in life. Some of them think me different from them and look at me as a foreigner, as an intruder, perhaps even an enemy. They don't see me with your eyes, but you see them through my eyes, and I am able to love them now the way you love them. My spiritual blood type is this faith that gives love, inspires love, empowers love, and ultimately, is love.

Dear God, you are not a mystery, you are a ministry that rules all hearts, all minds, all souls, from a leaf on the ground to the universe spread to infinity. Today, this moment, every moment, I give myself to you. From this day forward, I live my life in you and thus am lived by you.

JOURNEY OF KNOWLEDGE TO GOD
STAGE 3: ARRIVE

*See life as a school and all circumstance
as carrying opportunities to grow.
In this way, God expands you.*

Voice of God

There once was a kitten that had made up its mind to catch its tail. Day and night, this kitten ran circles, chasing its tail but to no avail. Finally, it tired itself and sat in misery, crying. An older cat was passing by, and upon seeing the sad kitten crying, approached it. "What's wrong, young one?" the cat asked. The kitten cried: "I have been trying to chase my tail for many days and nights, but I have been unsuccessful. This was my sole purpose in life, and now my life is unfulfilled." "Ahh," the cat mused. "I used to be just like you when I was young. I, too, thought it the purpose of my life to catch my tail. I, too, struggled for months trying to catch it. Finally, I gave it up." The wise cat continued: "Since the day I left chasing my tail, I have observed that the tail has been chasing me. Wherever I go, it chases me and doesn't leave me, even for a minute. I didn't need to chase it after all."[23]

The minute you were born, my child, you became two from one: the first being your essence, the real you, hence, my essence, the eternal you, and the second being your ego or temporal self. This ego gives you an identity based in the world, defined by your job, wealth, status, accomplishments, ethnicity, gender, religion, family, community, and so on. You have made it the purpose of your life to chase this ego and its desires. So you spend all your energy running the eternal after the temporal.

---

[23] Adapted from C.L. James, "On Happiness," in *To See a World in a Grain of Sand*, by Caesar Johnson (Norwalk, CN: C.R. Gibson Co., 1972).

Since the ego is immaterial, an illusion, no matter how much you run, the moment never arrives when it's realized. It continues to evade you, asking for more: more money, more houses, more jewelry, a bigger bank account, a bigger company, a better spouse.

Like the cat that had to stop chasing its tail, you have to stop chasing the ego. Thereafter, the eternal you embarks on its journey of life; it knows the way, and it is the way. Then, the ego follows you wherever you go. Life becomes a school with lessons to learn, and growth to experience—not only material growth, but also spiritual growth. You expand into higher states of being and living.

You can easily test which life you are living: the life of chasing your tail or letting your tail chase you. Whenever you experience any personal loss (such as loss of money, loss of health, loss of a job, loss of a dear one, loss of love, loss of respect), monitor your sense of self to see whether there's any question of "Why did this happen?" This "why" is focused on the problem: looking for blame, for someone to take responsibility, to hold accountable, and punish. Many times this blame is self-blame and slowly eats away at one's life. The ego loves this "why" because it allows it to further entangle you into chasing your tail. It relives this "why" over and over again to entangle you deeper and deeper.

If instead of "Why did this happen?" you find yourself asking "What can I now do about it?" then you are allowing the tail to chase you. This "what" is focused on the solution. It's looking for the learning behind the circumstance, to move oneself and others as quickly as possible into a better place of being— mentally, physically, and spiritually. There are no enemies of this "what," only friends who can further help. This "what" is not attached to yesterday, and how life was yesterday, and how that life is no longer today; rather, this "what" is focused on what life needs to be now so that it can become better. This "what" is not judging others, not judging the circumstances, not judging me, and above all, not judging oneself for making

27

mistakes. It accepts life wherever it is and moves forward to as better a place as possible.

Life is not envisioned to be filled with loss, my child. On the contrary, there is more gain than there is loss. But, the nature of the ego is always focused on the loss and never on the gain. I hear more complaints everyday than I hear gratitude from mankind. I feel more suffering everyday than I feel joy, even though there are more circumstances of joy in the life of man than that of suffering.

I am not denying that there are tragic circumstances in life that require thought, attention, and reflection. I am also not telling you to run away from your feelings. What I am telling you is to feel and respond to all of life's circumstances from the place of the eternal rather than the temporal. The eternal knows all, so it feels and responds from a place of peace and love. The temporal knows only itself, so it feels and reacts from a place of lack and pain.

I love you, my child, and I am always there showing and being the way. There are great lessons to learn in life, great adventures to live, and great spiritual capacities to develop. The material experiences and circumstances are only there to facilitate that spiritual development. They are as temporary as the effects of seeing death, loss, or sickness in a movie. Once the movie ends, the actor returns to his home, to his family, to be his real self. You, too, return to me once this life ends. There are other movies to be made, other lessons to learn, other roles to be played for each actor. So, live out this role completely, and courageously, while remaining connected with the actor within you, the eternal within you, living a life fully lived.

JOURNEY OF KNOWLEDGE TO GOD
STAGE 4: EXPERIENCE

Experience God as the author, source,
and destination of all life.
Everything and Everyone is from God,
in God, and through God.

Voice of Jesus Christ
(Jesus the Anointed One)[24]

It had been a long journey. I knew that the hour had come for me to depart from this world and return to my Father. There was an important teaching I had to deliver to my disciples before I left.

We were all sitting, eating the last meal that I would have with them. I decided it was time for that teaching and got up during the supper. I took off my outer robe and tied a towel around myself. I poured water into a basin and approached my beloved disciple Simon Peter.

Simon Peter was taken aback when he saw me approaching him. He asked me, "Lord, are you going to wash my feet?"[25] I replied, "You do not know now what I am doing, but later you will understand."[26] I knew that it was inconceivable for my disciples that I should wash their feet. But, the teaching I intended to give them couldn't be given any other way. I had to do the deed for them to truly understand.

Peter strongly resisted saying, "You will never wash my

---

[24] See John 13-14, to read more about "The Last Supper" of Jesus.

[25] John 13:6 (NRSV).

[26] John 13:7 (NRSV).

feet."[27] I felt Simon Peter's love in my heart. I heard him asking in his heart how he could allow his master to act like his servant. But, unless he allowed me to do this, he truly wouldn't take part, and share in this teaching with me. It's one thing to teach through words, yet another to teach by example. The example penetrates deeper and finds a home in the heart. I explained: "Unless I wash you, you have no share with me."[28]   Peter finally let me continue. One by one, I washed the feet of my disciples. One by one, I cleansed them of the physical dirt of the world.

After washing all their feet, I put on my robe and returned to the table. I explained: "Do you know what I have done to you? You call me Teacher and Lord—and you are right, for that is what I am. So if I, your Lord and Teacher, have washed your feet, you also ought to wash one another's feet."[29]

The temptations of the world are many. I had lived through these temptations myself. I had seen how those who claimed to be the Father's most devoted servants had submitted to these temptations. The biggest of these temptations is the idea that one is better than the other, and hence, deserves more than the other. The spirit had informed me how my own disciples had succumbed to this temptation earlier in the supper. Before I arrived, they had debated about who amongst themselves was the best in front of the Father.

The only way to safeguard them from this temptation was to plant an image in their heart of their master, their teacher, at their feet, cleaning their physical dirt. In the same way, they, too, must be willing to be at each other's feet. They, too, must clean the spiritual dirt that may accumulate while walking the way of God in this world. I continued to explain: "Very truly, I

---

[27] John 13:8 (NRSV).

[28] John 13:8 (NRSV).

[29] John 13:12-14 (NRSV).

tell you, servants are not greater than their master, nor are messengers greater than the one who sent them."[30]

God had been the sole authority in my life. I had felt him in my heart, and I had searched for him in the hearts and lives of all those with whom I convened. The Father was my Master and, I, his servant. Everything I did was through and with the will of my Father. It was my Father's will that I wash the feet of my disciples. It was my responsibility to reflect that will. I, as a servant and messenger, was not above my Father. My disciples, as servants and messengers of the same Lord, weren't above him either. We all must follow his will in all circumstances and reflect his nature: a nature of humility, of service, of healing and removing dirt and darkness from the being of mankind.

It was time for me to seal this teaching. I continued: "I give you a new commandment, that you love one another. Just as I have loved you, you also should love one another. By this everyone will know that you are my disciples, if you have love for one another."[31]

My entire life had been about this one word: "love." It had been so because I had loved my Father and had been loved by my Father. Through my Father's love, I had loved all of life. Truly, one who would follow my teachings would be one filled with love: love for himself, love for the other, and love for God. These aren't three separate loves but one same love as I demonstrated throughout my life. The only way that my disciples would keep me alive in their lives was if they kept the memory and example of this love alive. As they loved like I loved, they would love like the Father loves. He would come alive in their hearts, minds, and souls, as he had in mine. They would reflect his will, as I had reflected his.

Before we ended the supper, I reminded my disciples of this truth of giving one's life to God, and of having God come to

---

[30] John 13:16 (NRSV).

[31] John 13-34:35 (NRSV).

life in oneself. I told them: "The words that I say to you, I do not speak on my own; but the Father who dwells in me does his works. Believe me that I am in the Father, and the Father is in me."[32]

The time of my departure drew near. I knew that my teachings would always be with those who would seek the way upon which I walked. It is the way, the truth, and the life: not the life of the world, but the life of the eternal, infinite spirit.

---

[32] John 14-10:11 (NRSV).

JOURNEY OF KNOWLEDGE TO GOD
STAGE 5: RELIVE

O God, my life is your life and your life is my life.
Help me see you in all of life and all of life in me.

Voice of Shafeen

It was the summer of 2004. I was participating in a camp organized by my religious community called the "College Program on Islam." It was a two week residential program held at Bridgewater State University in Bridgewater, Massachusetts. I was there with many other youth from the ages of seventeen through twenty-five who desired a deeper understanding and experience of their faith.

The greatest epiphany during the program came when we were discussing the word "Islam." We learned that there were two ways to look at this word: first as a religion that applied to those who called themselves Muslims; second as a philosophy that applied to all of life. As a philosophy, the word stood for "submission to the will of God." In that context, any believer in God who submits to the will of God follows Islam and is a Muslim. So a Christian, a Jew, a Hindu, a Buddhist, if he/she is following the will of God, is a Muslim. In fact, all of nature, the birds, the trees, the clouds, the sun, they are all submitting to the will of God in their own way, praying in their own way, and following Islam and being Muslims in their own way.

This profound realization shook me at the core of my being. All along, I had been associating Islam with holding specific beliefs and following particular sets of rituals in line with those beliefs. Until then, I was a Muslim because I believed ABC and practiced XYZ. Instead I realized that Islam and true religion itself was less about believing and more about knowing. It was less about doing and more about being. But how would I know the will of God? Once having known it, how would I submit to that will (like the birds and the trees already were doing)?

As a teenager, when I would participate in school sponsored programs, which would require travel by bus, other young people would ask me, "Where's the bomb on the bus?" Next, they would laugh and I, too, would nervously smile back. They were poking fun at me for being a Muslim. Muslims were known for blowing up buses as well as buildings. Some who committed such acts sincerely believed that they were executing God's will. Was that God's will? Of course not! How could people be misled, then, to believe such a lie?

I realized that one's context, one's culture, and one's political, economic and life situation has a lot to do with how he/she understands and practices his/her faith. But all of these sources of faith were external based in the world. The will of God that I was searching for was more innate, more intuitive, and more natural. How could I find this will?

The answer came to me in the form of a greeting that I had often been exposed to but never truly understood. "Namaste," my Hindu friends would often say when greeting each other formally. The word spoke to my being and I searched for its meaning. That meaning was, "I bow to the divine in you." The dots started connecting fast. Of course, the trees and the birds and the clouds know the will of God because God resides in them. We, too, must know the will of God because God resides in us.

Most scriptures I read showed this to be true. In the Qur'an, God breathed his *Ruh* (literally spirit) into man before creation. In the Bible, God created man in his own image. In the Hindu scriptures, the *Atman* (soul) is a reflection of the *Parmatman* (God). So if we are all encoded with God in our essential being, why don't we follow his will?

As I explored further, the word "free will" kept popping up. God gave us free will so that we would choose to submit that will to him or choose to submit it to our temporal self, the ego. This was the eternal bet that God made with Satan that those who believe in God won't go astray and will truly submit to his will.

So the gift of free will became a curse. While it allowed us to show God's greatness, it also allowed us to show our own weakness. This is where I believe my brothers and sisters in Islam, who had committed those atrocities, had gone wrong. They had not submitted to the God within them. They had instead submitted to an idea of God and his teachings as articulated by certain others plagued by darkness within them. They weren't the only ones. Brothers and sisters from all religions through time and history had succumbed to notions of a vengeful and hateful God: a God built in the image of man. So rather than man reflecting God's image and expressing love and light, God was being limited to man's image and reflecting hate and war.

How could I make sure that I didn't succumb to such a temptation? It was a ritual of my faith that showed me the way. All Shia Ismaili Muslims, when they perform the prescribed daily prayer, go into a bow called *Sajda*, literally meaning "submission" or "prostration." A complete *Sajda* entails being on one's knees with the palms of the hands and forehead touching the ground. It had become customary for me to do this ritual with my head and not my heart. One day, my heart told me to bow in a complete *Sajda* and to not get up. I kneeled there for thirty minutes. In those thirty minutes, I submitted. I let go. I let go of knowing better than anyone else. I let go of knowing better than God. I decorated my free will in a lovely plate and presented it to my Lord. I said in my heart: "I give you back your gift, my Lord. It's better situated in your hands than mine. Take it from me and make it yours."

Days followed when I practiced this ritual again and again, sometimes for ten, sometimes for twenty, sometimes for thirty minutes: submitting, submitting, and submitting. It was easy to submit during the time that I was in *Sajda*. It was much harder to do the same, to keep my head down spiritually, when it was up physically, walking in the world.

Even today, I often find myself on the other end of a disaster caused by my free will. After a fight or an argument with a loved one, after displaying rudeness or anger with a coworker, or worse, with a stranger, I find myself saying, "Sorry Lord, I messed up, again." But the Lord is so kind, so loving. He always says, "It's okay, my son. This is not a destination, this is a journey, and you are on your way. I love you my son and I'll always be with you showing and being the way."

Truly, he's present especially before such disasters if I'm truly listening. Before I succumb to my ego, the Lord is there whispering, "You are better than this." What he's really saying is that "I am better than this. If you truly see me as you, and see my will as your will, follow my path of love, compassion, mercy, and forgiveness and become better than this." There are moments when I listen to that voice and become better. There are moments when I don't.

As the being of the Father penetrates me, takes over my will, I feel what he feels and see what he sees. He doesn't see difference like man sees difference. He sees himself in all of life as ultimate life. He loves all of life, even the ones who deny him. He serves all of life with all his heart, all his mind, all his soul and all his strength. He believes in his creation, believes in their submission, believes in their light, and believes in their salvation. He's waiting for each and every one of us to return to him, for we have come from him and to him is our return. He's perfect hope, perfect love, and perfect light. He is never judging, never impatient, never angry or upset. He's always available, always present, always showing and being the way to him through him. He reminds me: "All of life is in me and I am in all of life." I yearn for such a submission that I can be one with this truth and be in him like he's in me.

.

JOURNEY OF KNOWLEDGE TO GOD
STAGE 6: CONVERSE

My child, you are my life and I your life.
I breathe and witness all of life
through your being.

Voices of Man and God

Man: O God, if you are the stuff that life is made up of, why don't you make yourself known in a way that's undeniable? This way all will know that you exist instead of questioning your existence.

God: Ever since the beginning of time, I have made myself known in diverse ways. I first made myself known through nature. When man needed food, there was always food available through the trees, through the plants, through the roots. When man was thirsty, there was always water available through the many channels I created for him. Man witnessed the warmth and life that I provided through the sun. It's a sphere of hot gold that comes and goes every day in the perception of man. Though brilliant, it submits to a nature that supports man. Man has also seen the stars in the night, present for billions of years as existence beyond what man comprehends. Yet, man hasn't seen me through nature.

I made myself known to man through knowledge. I made available to man all sorts of knowledge that benefited him: the art of making fire, the art of growing wheat and other crops, the ability to build homes. Imagine how this knowledge must have reached the first man who ever utilized it. It was me, feeding him ideas in his head to try. Those ideas once utilized gave man what he would term the necessities of life. Yet, man didn't understand that these were gifts that came from me, from my heart and mind. Even today, I bestow creation after creation to you, ideas upon ideas to you, to make your life better. But you don't see me, you only see yourself and you only credit yourself.

I even sent my messengers and messages to you as proof of my being. Again and again they came to point all towards me. But you hurt them and killed them again and again. Even the messages that I sent with my messengers have been couched in history as man-made and believed by some and ignored by many.

So now I just wait until you have developed your own sense of being enough to see me in every aspect of life. This is the age and time when you are coming closer to doing that.

Man: O God, how can we know you simply in life? There are so many books and so many rituals. Is there a way to know you without having to read so much or understand so much?

God: Those who truly seek me know me in every moment and every second. I am the observer that watches the world from your eyes. I am also the observer that watches the world from universal eyes. In every moment, if you pay attention to the one watching, to the one observing, you are paying attention to me. The audience sitting in a movie theater watches the movie that plays in that theater. Who's watching the movie that's playing in your life? There's someone watching, processing, pondering, and wondering what to do about specific circumstances. There's someone expressing happiness and sadness at specific events. You associate your ego with all of this but your ego is truly a shell. It doesn't really exist.

From birth, someone tells you that you are "Mary" or "Victor" or "Vikram" and you believe them. They provide you with an ethnicity, a nationality, a culture, and the role that you play in society. All of you believe this as your identity, as your real self. But all of that is a shell with which society has identified you. The real you is the watcher, the one watching your movie of life, analyzing and interpreting it from a distance. That watcher is guiding you every moment on how to participate in the movie. When you lose yourself in the movie, you lose touch with the watcher. Then chaos is born, wars are fought, people are harmed, bad happens through man. When you are in touch with the watcher, with the God within, then peace, love, light, and compassion are born onto the plane of life, onto the movie of the individual concerned. It's that simple to know me from the inside, to know me as the watcher of the movie of your life.

To know me from the outside is not that difficult either. Pick up any leaf or flower. If you can't find a leaf or flower, pick up a grain of sand and ask: "Who created this? Who made this grain of sand the way that it is?" Obviously, the answer is nature, but who holds nature in its entirety so that nature can express itself? A human being has to breathe to live. A human being has blood that circulates throughout his body to give him the energy to live. Similarly, each flower, each plant, each grain of sand, has something that allows it to exist, to even hold its form. What's that thing which holds nature together? You often use glue to tape things together. What's the glue that holds all of life together? Of course, you'll say that it's molecules and the way they interact. But can you imagine billions and billions of molecules sticking naturally in so many different patterns to form life? This is impossible for you to do and yet nature does this all the time so easily. So, who's the one holding all of creation steady?

There's no one but me. I am the creator and the sustainer. I hold all of life in my hands. If for one second, I was to take my consciousness off any object, life would float away. Einstein, commenting on Quantum Physics and the enigma of consciousness turning a wave into a particle, once said: "I believe the moon is there even if nobody's looking."[33] I am the reason that the moon is there even if no one is looking because I am looking. I am the consciousness observing all of life and thus all of life is static or at least appears to be static.

Man: Dear God, what, then, constitutes a miracle? How is it that we experience and have the ability to experience miracles in our lives?

---

[33] Rosenblum, *Holos*, March 2007.

God: Miracles happen all the time, all around you. Miracles are simply instances where I have shifted or accelerated expected behavior for your benefit. As you pray to me with the expectation and feeling that I fulfill your prayers, I shift my consciousness so that I see a particular result set happening more than others. Each event has a possibility of happening. When my consciousness chooses to see the event of your desire, then that possibility is made real. But, you also have a lot to do with it for in you, I have also placed my consciousness.

You see, I am outside you but I am also within. So if you put your consciousness on the opposite of that event (for example, you pray for abundance but you concentrate on the idea that you are poor and nothing good ever happens to you), your consciousness influences or in many cases cancels my intent. Therefore, what you end up with is either nothing or something that's skewed towards my intent or your intent. This is why sometimes prayers appear to not be answered. I always answer your prayers.

Also, when you ask me for anything, it always translates to me into one thing: the "good." Sometimes however what you ask for is not good for you in the form that you have asked. So I put my consciousness on something else that is as good or better. I give that good to you as long as you don't cancel my intent. But you don't see that good when it manifests since you are looking only for the form for which you have asked. An example of this would be if you desired to have a certain someone as a partner in your life. But he/she is not good for you so I intend to bring another good person in your life. However, you are so stuck with the desire for the original person that you ignore this new person and continue to complain about your life.

Yes, bad things do happen in life. Some happen because you expect them to happen, as I described above. If you place your continuous focus and consciousness on a negative outcome, you manifest it in your life. Others happen because you have chosen to experience them for your soul's development before coming into this world. Yet another cause is the universal law of cause and effect—"what you sow, you reap"—what many refer to as *Karma*, whether it's at an individual or collective level. Finally, bad things happen in your life when you move away from the light, into darkness, and manifest that darkness through your words and deeds.

Experiencing miracles depends on you knowing and believing that I am present in every aspect of your life. I work 24/7 to better your life, to give you your heart's desires, to serve you completely. Life serves you completely in every way. Today, many have called this the *Law of Attraction*. But that implies that somehow you "attract" me and my blessings into your life. It's rather that you recognize and tune into my ever presence. Having tuned into that presence, you align with my abundance, with my nature as the grantor of all that you could ever desire. When that desire is good, good for you and all others who may be impacted, it manifests in your life as quickly as your belief in it being real.

Man: But God, why don't you do something about the suffering? Why are more people starving today than eating a normal meal? Why are more people dying of hunger and avoidable causes than ever before in history?

God: Have you felt or suffered the hunger or thirst of the people you mention above? Many times you ask questions without experience. You take numbers and statistics to be your source of knowledge. Experience the life of the people behind the statistics. Live with someone who's poor for a day. Spend some time with those dying of hunger and thirst. Your question will change. There are two reasons for that.

One reason is that you'll see the inner resolve of those who are hungry or dying. These people don't consider themselves as being starved or killed by God. Instead, they blame society, inequalities, and their governments for not doing what they are supposed to do. In that they are exactly right. I have provided enough food to feed your planet over six hundred times every day, even with today's population. But where's that food? Who withholds that food from the hungry?

You may ask then, why don't I instill my will and take away from those who are hoarding and give to those who are poor? The answer is free will. When I created man, I gave him free will to live his life the way he chose. This is where your free will has led you—away from me and away from your responsibility towards your fellow brothers and sisters. As humanity, you appear to be distinct but you are actually one, one soul, one life. This soul has chosen to allow suffering for itself with the expectation that other parts of it will come to its help. Therefore, the hungry suffer because in their souls, they wait for their fellow human beings to come to their aid. This is why they don't blame me—they blame their fellow human beings.

Another reason why your question on suffering will change is that you'll see that the hungry and dying lead very simple lives. They aren't worried about much except from where their next meals are coming. And when they find their meals, the smiles on their faces, the joy as they eat, the laughter that they share, it's more than all the years of happiness that one may enjoy as a millionaire. Their lives are a simple reflection of grace, joy, and gratitude. The gratitude in their hearts for getting a morsel of food is usually more than I receive from someone to whom I have given the riches of this world. In some senses, one may say that these people are better off, happier than most of the world. For in their small moments of happiness, they live out more joy than most of you get out of your entire lives. Who's really suffering, then? Who's really poor? Who's truly living?

JOURNEY OF KNOWLEDGE TO GOD
STAGE 7: REALIZE

*I now walk the road of my life
with clear knowledge to God.
There's no person, place, or state
in my life in which he's not.*

Voice of Reader

As I return back to my day to day life, I reflect on the following questions to apply lessons from this journey:

- What new insights did I receive through this journey about life and about God?

- What changes will I make in my daily life as a result of these new insights?

- How will these changes help me live a more fulfilled and meaningful life?

Journey of Purpose through God

God as the <u>*G*</u>*ate* <u>*of*</u> <u>*d*</u>*estiny*

I am nothing. He is all. I do nothing of my own. He does it. That is what I am, God's pencil. A tiny bit of pencil with which he writes what he likes. God writes through us, and however imperfect instruments we may be, he writes beautifully.

— Mother Teresa, *My Life For The Poor*

JOURNEY OF PURPOSE THROUGH GOD
STAGE 1: ASPIRE

Hear God calling you to your true life purpose.
That purpose is why you exist.

Voice of Shafeen

Once, a mystic was sitting on a wall next to a river. He noticed that a scorpion was walking near the edge and fell into the river. The mystic picked up the scorpion immediately to save its life. However, the scorpion became frightened, stung the mystic, and fell back into the river. The mystic again reached out and picked up the scorpion and again the scorpion stung him. This happened a few times until the mystic was able to finally get the scorpion out of the river onto the wall and guide it away from the edge. A witness asked the mystic: "Friend, you know that it is a scorpion's nature to sting. Why, then, did you continue to save it from drowning? The mystic replied: "Because, I also know that it is my nature to save."[34]

Today, more and more people are trying to find the meaning, the calling, the purpose of their lives. Everyone is looking for that gift, that talent, which they were born to bring onto the plain of life. Unhappy men and women are quitting their jobs and sometimes leaving their families and comfortable lives to pursue their calling. Though the aspiration of seeking fulfillment and one's purpose is noble, many times the perception is that this fulfillment resides out there in the world; hence, one believes that he/she has to travel great distances and sacrifice immensely to experience this purpose. "Pain is gain" is a motto that resonates with this type of searching for self-

---

[34] Adapted from John Suler, "The Nature of Things," Zen Stories to Tell Your Neighbors, accessed August 8, 2015,
http://truecenterpublishing.com/zenstory/onesnature.html.

fulfillment. As the mystic teaches us in the story, it may not even be necessary for us to go anywhere in order to serve our true purpose. We may be able to live out our true purpose wherever we are by being true to our own nature, to our own being, "in here." This is in contrast to meeting someone else's standard of our purposefulness "out there." The key is how we connect with what's "in here," to unveil our true nature, purpose, and calling.

In this journey of "Purpose through God," we strive to connect with the spirit of God "in here," within each and every one of us. Through that spirit, we strive to understand God's vision for our personal existence. Purpose is something that's hardwired in all of creation. The sun lights the earth and allows all life to find sustenance through it. The moon serves as a reminder of the sun in the night and causes the tides of the oceans. Trees bear fruits; clouds give rain; soil nurtures plants; wind allows for movement and migration. Everything that has been caused to exist has its own unique purpose or effect. In serving that purpose, each piece is a part of the bigger purpose of God as the creator and sustainer of all of life. Similarly, we, too, have our unique purpose. In serving that purpose, we, too, serve God's purpose for all of life. Accordingly, the best definition of God in this journey is GOD as the Gate Of Destiny.

The etymology of the word *destiny* comes from the Latin word *destinare*. This word can be broken into two words, "de" meaning "completely" and "stinare" meaning "to stand." To see God as the Gate of Destiny is "to completely stand" where God stands in the purpose or vision of one's life. God created each of us in his own image. Therefore, encoded in each of us is a purpose which reflects God's purpose, his essential and eternal nature. When we completely stand aligned with that purpose or nature of God within ourselves, we become an extension of him bringing his light into the world. Thus, man lives out man's destiny when he aligns with God's vision of man's life. In that same moment, God lives out God's destiny by living out his life, his purpose, through man. Purpose, in this way, is a collaborative exercise in which man expresses through God, and God expresses through man, on the plain of life. We witness this truth in the lives of the greatest of God's teachers who fulfilled their own purpose, while fulfilling God's.

One purpose of God is to guide and keep mankind on the right path. In the Qur'an, God teaches mankind a prayer: "Keep us on the right path. The path of those upon whom Thou hast bestowed favors. Not (the path) of those upon whom Thy wrath is brought down, nor of those who go astray."[35] One example of a teacher of God who fulfilled this purpose is the great philosopher Socrates. He guided the people of his time to the path of wisdom, truth and righteousness. He went around questioning people on the basis of what they held to be virtuous in their lives and in the life of the community. Through questioning and discussion, he was able to deconstruct the superficial beliefs and ideas of some of the most influential people of his time. He guided his people to turn to their souls for true wisdom and virtue rather than to the material world and its illusions of wealth, fame, and power.[36] Socrates taught that grounded in the virtues of the soul, one would lead a just and pious life. Having walked such a path in life, after death, one would join the virtuous and the pious, in the realm of the divine, immortal and wise.[37]

Another purpose of God is to protect and guard life. In the Old Testament, we are taught: "If you say, 'The Lord is my refuge,' and you make the Most High your dwelling, no harm will overtake you, no disaster will come near your tent."[38] We

---

[35] Qur'an 1:6-7 (Shakir).

[36] John M. Cooper, D. S. Hutchinson, eds., *Plato Complete Works* (Indianapolis, IN: Hackett Publishing Company, 1997), Apology 29e-30b.

[37] Cooper and Hutchinson, *Plato*, Phaedo 80d-81a.

[38] Psalm 91: 9-10 (ESV).

see this purpose in the life of the teacher, Krishna. Krishna protected and rescued all who turned to him for help. As a child, he performed miracles, such as lifting mountains, destroying demons, and turning away fires and storms in order to protect the people of his village.[39] Before the great battle of Mahabharata began, Krishna noticed the cry of a small bird who had built a nest on the turf in the middle of the battle field. Krishna moved that nest to the side of the battlefield. He covered it with a great elephant bell so that it wouldn't be affected by the eighteen days of battle. He fed the bird and her younglings daily so that they would survive. During the battle itself, he guided the side of the good against evil to victory.[40] In small and big ways, therefore, Krishna lived out God's purpose as the great protector of all of life.

Another purpose of God is to love and nurture life. In the New Testament, we are told: "Everyone who loves has been born of God and knows God. Whoever does not love does not know God, because God is love."[41] This love permeated the life of Jesus. He even loved all who most despised. He loved the poor, the crippled, the lame, and the blind. He healed the lepers whom no one would touch. He stood in the midst of accusers who wanted to stone a woman for adultery and said: "Let him who is without sin among you be the first to throw a stone at her."[42] While knowing that Judas, one of his own disciples, was going to betray him, Jesus still carried out the act of washing Judas' feet as he did the feet of his other disciples.[43] Even when

---

[39] Vanamali, *The Complete Life of Krishna: Based on the Earliest Oral Traditions and the Sacred Scriptures*, Rep. ed. (Rochester, VT: Inner Traditions, 2012), EPUB e-Book, pt. 1, chap. 6-8.

[40] Ibid., pt. 3, chap. 26-27.

[41] 1 John 4:7-8 (NIV).

[42] John 8:7 (ESV).

[43] John 13 (NIV).

the people of his time planned to punish him severely for this love, he said to God on their behalf: "Father, forgive them, for they do not know what they are doing."[44]

In this way, we see purpose emanate through the lives of each of God's teachers. God serves all of life through them, and they serve all of life through God. Hence, service is the greater purpose of these teachers and God. Service is also the destiny of each and every one of us as we aspire to live out our meaning of life, our calling, through God.

As we reflect on this truth in our lives, we may find ourselves asking the question, "What is the best way to serve?" The best way to serve, perhaps, is to be aware of opportunities to serve, not just in magnanimous ways, but also in small ways, every moment in our lives. We need to keep not just our eyes and ears open, but most importantly, our hearts open. Within our heart, the spirit "in here" notifies us when someone need's our service. As we are advised in the Old Testament: "Keep your heart with all vigilance, for from it flow the springs of life."[45] When we lack this awareness, we may miss an opportunity to serve a brother or sister in life. As we do, we may miss the opportunity to serve God within that brother or sister. God is present in every place and each being. So, when we serve one of his beings, we serve him; when we ignore or turn away from serving one of his beings, we ignore or turn away from him.

As we make ourselves available for God to bring his guidance, his protection, his love, into the lives of others, God expands our capacity to fulfill his mission. Sometimes, what we consider impossible for us to do becomes possible, for nothing is beyond the will and imagination of God. This is reflected in the life of Moses when he was given the task of freeing the Israelites. He hesitated and replied: "Who am I, that I should go unto Pharaoh, and that I should bring forth the children of

---

[44] Luke 23:34 (NIV).

[45] Proverbs 4:23 (ESV).

51

Israel out of Egypt?"[46] God responded to Moses: "Certainly I will be with thee; and this shall be a token unto thee, that I have sent thee."[47] The presence of divine will and guidance accompanied Moses wherever he went and empowered him to do God's works. The miracles that Moses carried out stand proof of that will and its guidance. The same becomes possible for us as we, too, trust the presence of the divine will and guidance in completing our work, in completing God's work.

As more and more people find their purpose through God, great examples of humanity are born, great saviors of mankind. Each of them is lit by the same flame that lights the universe. As this light does its work, we find ourselves living a better life, in a better planet, where each one serves the other. In that service, each one finds his/her true self, his/her true nature.

---

[46] Exodus 3:11 (KJV).

[47] Exodus 3:12 (KJV).

JOURNEY OF PURPOSE THROUGH GOD
STAGE 2: PREPARE

Recognize that when God created you, he created you to serve his creation. You are God's grace upon all of life.

Voice of Man

Dear God, why am I here? For what purpose did you send me to this life? I look around me, and I see so many choices. Which one am I to choose? There are doctors, engineers, school teachers, priests, and writers. There are filmmakers, actors, directors, photographers, artists, and sculptors. There are politicians, CEOs, managers, and entrepreneurs. There are waiters, stylists, barbers, babysitters, and service representatives. I see lots of people working, lots of people earning to raise families, and others aiming to be successful. Which way is right for me? In which direction must I turn to succeed in life?

Dear God, I'm afraid to make the wrong choice. I see so many people depressed and stressed out with their lives. There's a phenomenon now, labeled *Karoshi* in Japan, where people are literally dying from overwork. Einstein was right when he said: "It has become appallingly obvious that our technology has exceeded our humanity." Slavery has been abolished, but people are still enslaved to their work, to their image in society, to their perception that material life and material gain is the objective of life. Children are raised with the idea that they must be at the top of their class, at the top of their school, at the top of their university, at the top of all of life. There's one grave error in all of this: one is alone at the top. There's no one at the top with whom to share one's life. And life is only lived when it's shared with others. So, we have become a bunch of units without unity, humans without humanity.

Dear God, where must I turn to find your eternal wisdom showing me the direction of my life? There are so many voices blurting on the television, on my email, on my smart phone, through YouTube, Facebook, Twitter, and on tools and apps of all kinds. I'm surrounded by so much information that I'm unable to decipher inspiration.

"Look at what I ate for lunch!"

"My new boyfriend, isn't he cute?"

"I just made my first million!"

"I'm tired of all the homeless. Why don't they just get a job?"

These are just some of the headlines I read in my social network today. Where are you in all of this? Why aren't you messaging me? Why aren't you on LinkedIn? I have gone to your homes to find you, but there I'm often made to feel like a lost child, a disobedient child, an unwanted child. I'm made to feel like I have strayed far, far away from my father's calling. How can I go far from something I don't even know about?

Dear God, save me from my own darkness, from my own confusion. Without your light to give me purpose, I'm called to all kinds of darkness—all readily available—sometimes in clear sight, inviting me in. "Have a drink; it will soothe you. Have a smoke; it will clear your mind. Shoot it up; you'll feel like you have never felt before." They have friendly faces, but once befriended, I see the darkness emerge. They eat one from within until nothing is left but an empty shell. Please help me find the light.

Dear God, I now sit in silence seeking your guidance … My heart stirs as I remember a story I had forgotten:

Once, a man searched for the purpose of life and went into a forest to meditate. One day, he observed an injured fox with a broken limb. The fox was handicapped and couldn't do much for itself. The man thought that the fox would surely die in such a state. The next moment, a tiger brought food for the fox. Every day, the man noticed that the tiger would share his food with the fox. In this way, the fox stayed alive. The man thought: "Surely, if God can provide for this fox, he can provide for me." So he sat under the tree meditating, waiting for some channel from God to bring him food. He sat, and sat, and sat, and no one arrived. He was hungry but stubborn and continued to wait. Just when he was about to pass out from hunger, he heard a voice from within: "My child, I intended for you to be like the tiger, not the fox."[48]

Dear God, it was as if I was looking for a match to light my life, and this story gave me the eternal flame. I finally understood the purpose of my life. I was created to serve. I was created to be of use to my fellow brothers and sisters. All my life, I have been looking to you like the handicapped fox. I have been waiting for someone to save me and have been complaining about why help never arrived. All my life, you have been waiting for me to act like the tiger that you have created me to be, that you have gifted me to be.

Dear God, there's so much I have to give to life. You have given me a smile that I can give freely to anyone and everyone with whom I come in contact. You have given me speech with which I can greet and spread words of love and light among those with whom I live. You have given me ears to be attentive to the needs of the suffering so that I can serve them best. You have given me eyes with which I can witness your light so that I can show it to those who remain in the dark. You have given me arms with which I can lift my falling brothers and sisters. You have given me legs with which I can walk them into safety and security.

Dear God, I was looking for a livelihood as the purpose of my life. What I now realize is that life itself is my purpose. Today, I'm thankful for this life, for this opportunity to serve and make a difference. Though I may have rainy days, I'll never let them douse the flame of my spirit. I'll never doubt my purpose again, my Lord. Wherever I am, the spirit of service will live in me and uplift all of life.

---

[48] Adapted from Anthony De Mello, S. J., "The Disabled Fox," in *The Song of the Bird*, 2nd ed. (Anand, India: Gujarat Sahitya Prakash, 1982), 97.

JOURNEY OF PURPOSE THROUGH GOD
STAGE 3: ARRIVE

*Imagine yourself as having the infinite power
and wisdom to grant one gift to the world.
God has sent you to deliver this gift.*

Voice of God

The mystic Rabia was once visited by two notable men. It
was a custom to offer the best food to one's guests. Rabia lived
a simple life and didn't have much food to offer. She put two
loaves of bread, all the food that she had, in front of her guests.
That instant, a beggar came to Rabia's door, asking for food.
Immediately, Rabia took the two loaves and gave it to the
beggar. Knowing that Rabia was a poor woman, the guests now
wondered what they would eat. Some moments later, a servant
girl visited Rabia and offered her eighteen fresh loaves of bread
sent by the girl's mistress, a lover of mystics. Rabia refused the
bread, insisting that there must be some mistake. There was,
since the servant girl had stolen two loaves of bread for herself.
She went away and returned with all twenty loaves. Rabia
graciously accepted the bread and offered them to the two men.
The guests knew some miracle had unfolded and asked Rabia to
enlighten them. She explained that as she was offering them the
two loaves, she worried about feeding them such a meager
meal. That instant, the beggar arrived. She offered the two
loaves of bread to the beggar firmly believing that God would
repay her ten-fold. When the servant girl only came with
eighteen loaves, she knew this was not the Lord's will, so she
waited until the twenty loaves arrived.[49]

Nothing pleases me more, my child, than your service to

---

[49] Adapted from A. J. Arberry, trans., *Muslim Saints and Mystics* (Ames, IA:
Omphaloskepsis, 2000), 34-36.

your brothers and sisters in life. I have created you so that you may know yourself, and the best way to know yourself is to see yourself reflected in the hearts of all whom you serve. Whom you are actually seeing through your service is me, both within yourself, and within all of life. This is the secret of closeness with me that my beloved spiritual children have known for thousands of years.

I have planted this secret deep in your heart. Whenever you serve, your heart tells you through the joy you feel that you have touched the veil of something very deep inside your heart. You don't have to serve in magnanimous ways to unearth this secret; rather, you have to dare, to intend, to make someone else's life a little better, a little brighter.

Whatever help you ask of me in this service will be granted. I'll come to your aid to make sure that you are able to fulfill your gift, and hence my gift, to mankind. As you serve without expectation of any reward or recognition, you'll feel your heart open. You'll feel my heart peeking through your heart. As you give yourself to life, you'll give yourself to me. As you give yourself to me, you'll give yourself to life.

There are many of you who are looking to serve me through a vocation, a career path. But your vocation serves you more than it serves me. It provides an opportunity for you to earn a living and have a good physical quality of life. My abundance is with you as you strive to find a good vocation to meet your needs, to exercise your passions, and to fulfill your dreams. But to serve me is much simpler than a vocation.

You serve me every moment you give yourself to life. This can happen at home when you are with your parents, siblings, spouses, or children. This can occur at work when you are with your co-workers, or on the road, or at a party, or a place of worship, or in nature. As you give yourself to life, you draw close to me in your heart, and to my purpose as the sustainer of all of life. Thereafter, I unveil a gift from your heart. That gift benefits whoever is in your presence. Sometimes that gift is a kind word, sometimes a check for a donation, sometimes a shoulder to cry on, and sometimes loaves of bread given to a hungry brother or sister. Know that these gifts, which come from me and come through you, are intended from the deepest spaces of your heart where I live. This is the purpose why you are here in this life. This is why you were sent, my child.

When my children give themselves to me increasingly, and through me, give themselves to their brothers and sisters, I make them a blessing upon mankind. These are the people you celebrate today—masters, teachers, change agents—who brought goodness, and therefore, Godliness, into their lives and the lives of all whom they touched. They unveiled the secret of service in their hearts and realized true closeness and friendship with me. It's my wish, my aspiration, to see you, also, do such great works and unveil that secret. It's my wish, my aspiration, to see you shine brighter than all the stars in the sky.

But a secret is only a secret when it remains unspoken. If you serve with the objective of worldly recognition, then you divulge my secret. The meaning and feeling of true service is diminished. In order to preserve this secret, know yourself as me, and know everyone you serve as me also, for that's true reality. Does the leg ever need to thank the hand for scratching an itch? Similarly, I don't need life to thank me, and knowing yourself as me, neither will you. This doesn't mean that you may not be publicly recognized, praised, or appreciated for your service. What this means is that your service will be independent of that recognition and my secret, and your service will be safe.

I love you and I am always with you, my child. There is never a moment when I don't live in you and live through you. So, live courageously, live without fear, don't be scared, don't be afraid, don't be worried, and don't be stressed. You are never in darkness, my child, even when it's night. The inner sun resides in your being and lights your world brighter than the outer sun ever could. Live your life as a blessing filled with love and light. Be grateful for each moment you live and live it fully.

JOURNEY OF PURPOSE THROUGH GOD
STAGE 4: EXPERIENCE

Experience your calling in action
delivering your gift and changing the world.
God creates every second in small and big ways.

Voice of Moshe Rabbeinu
(Moses Our Teacher)[50]

As per the Lord's wishes, we were encamped by the sea. As the Lord predicted, the Pharaoh came marching with all his forces: the horses, the chariots, the warriors with their swords drawn, thirsty for the blood of my people. Truly, it was a terrifying site, and my people began to wail. I encouraged them: "Do not be afraid. Stand firm, and you will see the deliverance the Lord will bring you today. The Egyptians you see today, you will never see again. The Lord will fight for you; you need only to be still."[51]

Though this pacified them, I remained troubled. I cried to the Lord within me: "Dear Lord, what do we do now? You have led us this far. Please don't let us now be overwhelmed. We are at your mercy, completely at your mercy. Save us, my Lord." The Lord replied in my heart:

Why are you crying out to me, Moses? You know what I have promised you, and I'll fulfill that promise. Tell my children to move forward. Raise your staff, and stretch out your hand over the sea to divide the water so that they can go through the sea on dry ground. I'll prevent the Pharaoh

---

[50] See Exodus 3 and Exodus 14, to read more about "Moses and the Burning Bush" and "Crossing the Red Sea," respectively.

[51] Exodus 14:13-14 (NIV).

and his men from reaching you.

That instant, the pillar of cloud that had been our guide in front of us moved behind us. Fear and confusion gripped the Pharaoh's army. They were prevented from coming any closer.

As the Lord had commanded, I raised my staff and stretched out my hand over the sea. Until that day, I had seen the Lord bestow sign upon sign, miracle upon miracle. In manifold ways, the Lord had showed his love for me and my people. But, what I witnessed next was larger than anything I had ever seen. A strong east wind pushed up against the sea and drove it back so that the waters literally split into two. As the Lord had promised, we crossed on dry land, with a wall of water on our right and another wall on the left. All night, the wind blew, and all night we made our way as quickly as possible to the other side.

I helped my brothers and sisters cross the sea. Even though there was urgency to this matter, my heart couldn't resist reflecting on my journey until that momentous day. I was a slave, who had turned into a prince, who had later turned into a shepherd. That shepherd would often think about his people and their distress but could do nothing to help them. That lowly shepherd would have lived out a quiet life in the desert if the Lord had not summoned him to his purpose.

One day, the Lord called me through a burning bush to free my brothers and sisters from the enslavement of the Egyptians. He had heard their cry, had felt my intention to help them, and had decided that the time had come for the oppression of the Egyptians to end. I remembered my utter disbelief in the Lord's choice, that I, a lowly shepherd, would deliver this task. I had no army, no wealth, and no kingdom. Upon whose authority would I ask the Pharaoh to let my people go? The Lord had replied: "I am the God of your father, the God of Abraham, the God of Isaac, and the God of Jacob. ... I will be with you."[52]

Truly, my Lord had been with me and had proven his glory and his love. He had raised me to a power unimagined. Though everything was done by the Lord, what the Egyptians, and even my own people heard and saw, were my voice and my hands. I had become the object of both blame as well as affection, loved as well as feared. Only I knew the complete truth: I was a mere instrument in the hands of the Lord.

Tears rolled down my cheeks as I helped the last of my people safely cross the sea. Night had turned into day and sunlight was breaking through the sky. Though across, my people were still afraid for their lives. The pillar of cloud had moved and the Pharaoh and his army had rushed into the bed of the sea in pursuit. They still desired to take their revenge on my people. The Lord jammed their chariots onto the bed of the sea and drove them into awe and confusion. The time had come for their terrible reign to end. As the Lord commanded me in my heart, I lifted my arms, and the sea flowed back into place. The Pharaoh and his army were utterly destroyed in that moment.

A great peace overtook all of my people. They had been rescued from the jaws of death by their Lord, working through his servant, Moses. I could see the light of his faith on their faces. It had been a long time coming, but I could also see rays of hope as they looked forward to their freedom and sang songs of joy and gratitude. I felt my heart open as a deeply desired wish reached fruition. One journey was complete, but my service to the Lord, and through the Lord to his children, had just begun.

---

[52] Exodus 3:6-12 (NIV).

JOURNEY OF PURPOSE THROUGH GOD
STAGE 5: RELIVE

*O God, I serve myself best when I serve you best
and I serve you best when I serve life best.
Service is why I exist.*

Voice of Shafeen

It was Friday evening, September 28, 2001. I was in Orange County, California, standing on the side of the 405-North Freeway (one of the busiest freeways on one of the busiest nights of the week). A few minutes prior, my car had been sideswiped by another and had spun out of control. After spinning twice, my car had come to a stop facing the opposite way on the freeway. One of the passersby had stopped and given me a ride to the side of the freeway where I now waited. The police arrived shortly. It took a few minutes for me to evaluate what had happened. The more I reflected upon the accident, the luckier I felt.

There were a total of three cars in the accident: my car, a second car that had sideswiped me, and a third that was hit when the second car also lost control. The other two cars landed in a ditch on the side of the freeway and were completely totaled. One of the drivers needed medical attention and was escorted away by an ambulance. I was a little shaken up but other than that, I had no scars or pain.

When the policeman approached me and looked at my car, his first question was, "Where did you get hit?" Both of us had to search for a few minutes before we found a spot, 3 by 5 inches, the size of a normal index card, where I had been hit. "Will your car start?" he asked. I had no idea. In the confusion after the accident, I had left my car in the middle of the freeway. The police had pushed and steered the car to the side. When I started the engine, I was surprised because the car was able to run. I was able to drive home that night. Soon, I realized that I had not been lucky; I had been saved that night.

A few months before, I had graduated from college and had joined one of the top technology consulting firms in the nation. It was my first exposure to consulting and I soon learned and enjoyed their motto, "We work hard but we play harder." I had just joined the firm but had already started dreaming of making it to partner one day. It was all about becoming a high performer as well as impressing the right people to rise quickly up the ranks. All my life until that point, even when away from home, my focus had been my faith and my family. These took a backseat as I focused solely on my career and social life. I had even started drinking, something that I had previously avoided since it was against my religion. Now I drank in order to fit in better with my colleagues and to have more fun at social events. The night that I had gotten into the accident, I had missed special evening prayers at my place of worship. Instead, in order to network, I had attended a dinner with senior executives from my firm and the client's. Fortunately for me, it had not been a drinking night otherwise the accident could have been a big disaster.

The months that followed the accident were filled with a lot of reflection and "what if?" scenarios. I had spun twice on the busiest freeway on the busiest night of the week and had hit nothing else, not even the median. Someone was looking out for me. It had been years since I had talked to this someone in my heart. I felt very restless and needed to hear from him. For years, I had not attended to my connection with him. This made hearing from him very difficult.

That December, I visited my sister in Atlanta, Georgia. My brother-in-law would attend morning prayers every day at our place of worship which included meditation from 4:00 a.m. to 5:00 a.m. He motivated me to join him. I accompanied him, listening to recordings of *Waez* or faith-based talks, on our drive there. Once there, I would meditate on the word *Ya Ali*, one of the names of God in the Muslim faith. This has always been the name of God that resonates deep in my heart. It means, "He who is above all else."

After seven days of meditation, I experienced an opening. The Lord spoke to me from the depths of my being. He had very simple instructions. "I am sending you an opportunity to serve in the next month. Take it." That was all. Though the instructions were brief, accompanying them was a strange peace that permeated my being. The restlessness, which had taken over after the accident, was gone.

I was offered an opportunity to serve in my religious community the next month. I said yes. After that opportunity, another and then another came. I said "yes" again and again. I served publicly as well as anonymously, with youth as well as adults: teaching faith, counseling troubled teens, helping at sports tournaments, planning and administering national and local initiatives, designing community databases, cleaning and vacuuming our place of worship, helping people park at fundraising events, reviewing college application essays, performing on stage for inter-faith initiatives, facilitating sessions to improve parent-teen relations, writing plays, training mentors and teachers, holding college mixers, and giving faith-based talks and presentations. *Seva*, the term we use in our religious community for devotional service to the Lord and to his children, became the purpose of my life. As my service grew, so did my relationship with the Lord. He spoke with me often in my heart and provided me clarity in my service and in my life.

Though I had served locally and nationally for my religious community, I didn't experience the essence of *Seva* until a special elder came into my life. At one point, she had been a leader in my religious community. As she got older, she faced many trials and tribulations. She didn't have much family surrounding her and lived alone in a senior community apartment. She lived twenty-five minutes away from our place of worship but desired to attend as often as possible. There was a ride schedule drawn up and different volunteers were approached so that the responsibility of transporting her wouldn't fall on one person. I was assigned one day a week to transport her for evening prayers at our place of worship.

While giving her a ride, the volunteer had to be very careful not to upset her. She was very hot-tempered and just disagreeing with her on a topic of discussion could lead her to lose her cool. She was also quick to notice if a volunteer was rude or inattentive to her needs in anyway. In that case, she would scold him harshly, regardless of who was around or where it occurred. One had to keep her informed of when she would be picked up and dropped back home and be prompt at both times. She also needed help getting in and out of the car, buckling seat belts, and climbing up and down the stairs. One had to show diligence in giving her this help. There were rare occasions when she smiled or laughed and those were the most endearing moments. She truly had a beautiful smile, and when she laughed, she laughed like a child. But her general demeanor made her very unpopular at our place of worship. Most people preferred not to talk to her or deal with her in anyway.

It was on an occasion when I was assigned to give her a ride and help her that she changed my understanding and experience of service forever. We had just arrived at our place of worship. I walked over to her side of the car and helped her get out. I held her hand and walked with her to the stairs. As I usually did, I climbed a step ahead of her and pulled her up the stairs, one step at a time. In the middle of the stairway she stopped. I looked at her and asked, "Everything okay?" She looked back at me, and gave me one of those beautiful rare smiles. She spoke slowly: "You know, yesterday, the Lord came to me in my dreams. He asked me something. He asked me: 'When I come to visit, will Shafeen help me up the stairs like he helps you?' I told him, 'Of course Lord, he definitely will.'"

Her words struck my heart. As I continued to help her up the stairs, I asked the Lord in my heart, "Dear Lord, what does this mean?" The Lord replied: "Don't you understand, you already are helping me up the stairs. Every time, you lift her up the stairs, you lift me also. Every time, you serve her, you serve me also. Your service to any one of my children is your service to me."

Tears welled up in my eyes as I got back in my car to go home and pick up my family for worship. For the longest time, it was an unpleasant chore to help this elder. For the first time, I realized the blessing it had really been. She had taught me true humility and commitment in my service. She had pushed me to strive for excellence in the smallest service like opening a car door or holding a hand or helping her climb the stairs. Most importantly, she had taught me the lesson—when I served her, I wasn't serving her; I was actually serving the Lord.

The Lord doesn't always appear in a heavenly form with beautiful music playing in the background as we may expect. Sometimes the Lord appears in the form of those who are marginalized and excluded. Consequently, they are filled with anger and bitterness. Do we have the courage to serve him regardless of how he appears to us? When we do, we find him reflected in our being and also in those whom we serve. Thereafter, the secret of service illumines our heart and the essential purpose of life is fulfilled.

Truly, that accident on the 405-North freeway had saved my life: not just my physical life, but my spiritual life. As I served the Lord by serving his children, I found my purpose in life. That purpose opened a world to me that I never knew existed.

JOURNEY OF PURPOSE THROUGH GOD
STAGE 6: CONVERSE

My child, service is your purpose
to me and through me.
Life has been intended to serve itself.

Voices of Man and God

Man: O God, I'm still not clear about my purpose. What am I here to do?

God: When I created the world, I created each of you, my spiritual children, in my own image. In that moment, your purpose and my purpose became one, to serve my creation. The best way for me to serve my creation is for me to express my creativity. The same is true for you. Each and every one of you has the potential to create your life just like I have created all life. In this way, not only do you serve yourself but you serve all of creation as well. This, of course, means that you must create with the same love with which I created. This, also, means that as you create, you must harness the divine potential within you, and you must be tuned to the divine command in you.

Now you may ask, "If I have the potential to create just about anything, what should I create?" This question is very similar to having a genie that grants you three wishes and you have to decide which three to choose. The more specific you are, and the more you believe that your wishes will come true, the easier it is for the genie to fulfill these wishes. Mankind is filled with a spectrum of wishers and creators. Some only want to create for themselves and wish for something specific but don't believe in their hearts that it will come true: "Give me a million dollars!" "Give me a huge house next to the beach!" "Give me a fast car that goes from 0 to 60 miles per hour in less than three seconds!" Others want to create for the world but pick a problem that's too big for them to solve and too general for the genie to grant: "I want to solve world hunger!" "I want peace all over the world!" "I want to end global warming!" Then there are those who are in the middle, creating for themselves or others, at a level of specificity as well as belief in its reality: "I desire a job that will allow me flexibility to work from home." "I want to meet a good life partner who will think from the heart, rather than the head." "I would like to create a social organization providing guidance and support to the poor to help them move out of their poverty." Those people are usually the ones who succeed in manifesting their creativity. But are they truly focused on that which gives them joy? Do they ask for that which exercises their potential as well as fulfills their responsibility towards their fellow brothers and sisters?

Now you may ask, "What gives me joy?" When I refer to joy, I am not talking about the immediate joy or contentment of eating your favorite ice cream. That's a great way of coming to a place of appreciating life if one is filled with regret and despair. What I am talking about is long-lasting joy. What activity, when done by you, provides long-lasting joy? What activity creates more fun than worry about the time or energy you are expending? In such creativity lies the answer to your purpose. That activity is the answer. But some may come back and say: "I enjoy rock climbing. This is when I feel one with nature and have the most lasting joy."

The problem with this answer is that you only experience joy in rock climbing <u>while</u> you do the activity. In that regard, rock climbing is very similar to the ice cream I talked about earlier in which you have joy <u>while</u> eating the ice cream. When I refer to an activity that gives you joy, I am talking about something deeper. What do you do before which you have enthusiasm and passion, and after which you experience bliss and joy which lasts for a long time, which creates an anticipation to do it again? The joy must be present not only during the activity but before and after it, as a sign, as a homing signal, that you have arrived.

Find that activity, that creativity, in your life. It will usually involve serving not just yourself but others. It will usually involve inner growth not just within yourself but also within others. It will usually be measured in terms of quality vs. quantity; whether you impact two people or two million people, the joy would be the same.

Man: O God, many people are unable to live out their joy. They are raising families, paying bills, doing jobs or running businesses that make them unhappy but support their kids and families. What do you have to say to those people?

God: I have allowed you to create your life in whatever way you desire. Working to support one's family and to pay one's bills can take one of two forms: "life uplifting" or "life denying." Below are these two forms along with a sample of inner thoughts that reflect each state:

Life Uplifting – I was created to improve the lives of my family. So I go to work expecting to do good work. I try to help others and make a difference every day. This way, I spread happiness at my work and experience joy from it. I also make a good living which allows for me and my family to have a good quality of life. My life is worth living. My work plays an empowering and fulfilling role in my life.

Life Denying – I hate my work. I hate the people I work with. I'm stuck in my role and have no sense of growth or learning or joy from my work. But my work pays me a lot of money and so I'm stuck here. No other place would pay me this much. I need to sustain all the activities, all of my family's expenses. They are counting on me to make this money, so they can have a good life.

It's possible that people that you describe are within a spectrum of feelings or emotions about their work in between the two forms that I have discussed above. The closer they are to "life uplifting," the better life they live for themselves and for

69

others. In that case, they are living out their purpose because their purpose, their creativity, is serving their family as well as their customers, clients, and coworkers. In serving those people, they find joy. Sure, every day is not golden at home or at work but these people choose to see the light rather than the darkness. These people are happy in their families and at their work.

The closer people are to "life denying," the more recipe for disaster they are cooking in their life. They associate the happiness of their families with money or with their family's material needs. They also perceive themselves as sacrificial lambs to fulfill those needs. This is very dangerous. Subconsciously, this leads one to despise his/her life and the family who "forces" him/her to live such a life. The family on the other hand is shown a model of life that prioritizes material needs, such as money, above the simple joys and happiness of life. Therefore, they end up valuing people, inner fulfillment, time with each other, and love for each other, less and valuing money, cars, homes, and status, more. This creates a self-fulfilling hell for all involved. The caregiver in this case lives an unfilled life. The care-receivers in this case become like the caregiver when they themselves grow up associating material needs above spiritual ones.

If this is your life, you need to go into solitude and reflect on what your life has become and why. When you realize the truth, and find the passion and focus to change your life to "life uplifting," then you'll be able to break down the barriers of material need and greed for yourself and your family. It will take time for everyone to adjust to the new way of life but life takes care of itself.

I'll say one general thing in this regard. When you serve others with a feeling of regret or despair or any negative feeling, you aren't serving but hurting others and yourself. Service is not just deed, it is word, it is thought, it is energy and vibration. When you serve effectively, you add love and light into a space of fear and darkness. But when you are filled with fear and darkness yourself, you add even more darkness to the existing void. It's better for you to earn less, and offer a lower quality of material life to your family, and be happy doing it, rather than earning a lot, and offering your family the world, and be sad or angry doing it. When you are sad or angry, that feeling will spread throughout your family, and you'll be hurting them unconsciously. You'll also be modeling an example of fear, greed, competition, continuous struggle and despair, for your kids. They, too, will fall into that conditioning when they grow up to be adults.

It's so much better to live a simpler life and have more joy, love, and appreciation. It's so much better to have more laughter and more hugs, while living in a small house, driving a small car, or having a small bank account. I'll not forsake you. As long as you have the intention to take care of your family, I'll provide for your every need. I promise you, if you are willing to do your share, food and work will find you and so will joy and appreciation. As you sleep every night, the peace that you will feel in your heart will be priceless.

Man: O God, there are those who are fulfilling their calling, and yet are unhappy. They are struggling to make ends meet. Sometimes their own families have pushed them aside, calling them failures. What would you say to those people?

God: When you follow your calling (when I say calling, I mean the deepest desire of your heart that is an agent of change, not just for your life but the lives of others) with all your heart and all your soul, then, there's no turning back. Then no ONE is really yours and EVERYONE is yours. Then you are operating from a divine point of view, from a divine perspective, and such a perspective is super-empowering. This perspective doesn't care about material gains. It doesn't care about quantity or quantifiable difference. It only cares about compassion, love, hope, empathy, seeing oneself and others in the best of light, and seeing life in the best of light.

People who espouse such a perspective will usually face trials and tribulations for two reasons. First, because some of these trials are just their lot of life, circumstances and events that they themselves have identified pre-birth, to learn from life. Second, because such people will usually break down barriers of society, barriers that have been erected sometimes for thousands of years, barriers that are part of the society's norm. These barriers keep people from helping, loving and supporting others. Those who follow their calling challenge these barriers and norms, like my messengers did, and strive to raise society to a new norm. Because they run against the norm, they suffer. Society may discourage them by putting a lower monetary value on that work. See the plight of the teachers and the social workers in your society today. But those who are true to their hearts will persevere and will rise above the societal resistance.

Ultimately, I'll not forsake those who are close to my heart. Those who follow their own hearts in serving others are the closest to my heart. I'll make sure that their homes are well lit, that their families are sheltered, that there's food on the table every day. Even if their families forsake them, I'll support them by sending them my friends to encourage them, to empower them, to show them my light and love. It's through these special ones that life is sustained, that this universe continues to be a universe of God, and of good. As long as they have hope, they have faith, these special ones will find my light, will find inner fulfillment. Even while struggling, they'll have joy in their hearts and be happy.

There are many examples of such people that have walked in your time, people like Mother Teresa, Martin Luther King, Jr., and Gandhi. They have found ultimate fulfillment while having an immense impact on their lives and the lives of others.

JOURNEY OF PURPOSE THROUGH GOD
STAGE 7: REALIZE

I now climb the mountain of my life
with clear purpose through God.
I serve him by uplifting
my brothers and sisters in life.

Voice of Reader

As I return back to my day to day life, I reflect on the following questions to apply lessons from this journey:

- What new insights did I receive through this journey about life and about God?

- What changes will I make in my daily life as a result of these new insights?

- How will these changes help me live a more fulfilled and meaningful life?

Journey of
Presence in God

God as the
Guru of detachment

If you abandon your ego, you become God or Buddha! When you let go of everything, when you have shed everything, when you have finished with your own personal consciousness, then you are God or Buddha. ... But if you tell yourself, 'Now I have abandoned everything and I am God,' if you think you are God, then you aren't God at all.

— Taisen Deshimaru, *Questions to a Zen Master*

JOURNEY OF PRESENCE IN GOD
STAGE 1: ASPIRE

Let go of everything so that you can rest in God.
Resting in God is most productive.

Voice of Shafeen

A mystic had just left a forest and had reached the outskirts of a village. He noticed a man wildly running from the village and coming towards him. As the man came close, he yelled, "The stone, the stone, please give me the stone." The mystic questioned, "What stone?" The man answered: "Last night, the Lord came to me in a dream. He told me that if I went outside the village at dusk, I would find a mystic who would give me a precious stone that would make me rich forever." The mystic rummaged in his sack and pulled out a huge diamond. "He probably meant this one. I found it yesterday in a ruin in the forest. It's yours if you so desire." The man took the stone home and tossed and turned all night assessing the riches that he had inherited. At the break of the next morning, he returned to the same spot and found the mystic. Holding out the stone, he requested the mystic: "Give me, instead, the wealth inside of you that allows you to give away this stone."[53]

Today, we live in a materialistic world. In it, everyone is chasing the next best thing. For some, it's the next home, the next car, the next promotion. For others, it's the next iPhone, the next tablet, the next video game. As we invest our thoughts, our lives, deeper and deeper, in this material-chasing world, we either feel more and more overwhelmed or more and more empty. We may feel overwhelmed, trying to protect what we have gained so that we don't lose it. We may feel empty

---

[53] Adapted from Anthony De Mello, S. J., "The Diamond," in *The Song of the Bird*, 2nd ed. (Anand, India: Gujarat Sahitya Prakash, 1982), 182-183.

because no matter how much we gain, we never feel complete, whole, fulfilled, and happy. Every new toy becomes old, and the toy chasing never ends. In such an environment, we need the wealth that the mystic has, the wealth that allows him to give up the chase, to give away the toys, and let go of the material. The mystic has eternal fulfillment because he's present in the spiritual rather than in the material, in the eternal rather than in the temporal.

In this journey of "Presence in God," we strive to find presence in the background upon which all of life unfolds: God. God is the creator of all of life; hence, he's a point of existence and awareness that's above and yet within all of life. When we connect with his presence in our inner being, we are able to see our physical life as a mere punctuation mark in the larger spiritual life. Thereafter, all the problems, all the difficulties of life, seem very small and distant. We experience detachment from our physical life. Accordingly, the best definition of God in this journey is GOD as the Guru Of Detachment.

The word *Guru* originates from two syllables in Sanskrit: *gu* meaning "darkness" and *ru* meaning "removal." As a *Guru*, God removes the darkness and leads us towards the light. In this journey, God leads us to the light, and therefore knowledge and experience, of detachment. Through this detachment, we strive to "Let go and let God": let go of all the problems of the past and worries of the future; let God take care of all of them in his way at his time. This requires us to loosen our attachment or association with our temporal self, our ego, and merge into our eternal or Higher Self, the spirit of God within. We hear these teachings referred to today by phrases, such as "being in the present moment" or "being in the now." Though the collective humanity may be waking up to this message recently, this is a timeless message that has been part of many ancient teachings and the lives of ancient teachers.

Krishna describes this Higher Self when he says: "The Self cannot be pierced by weapons or burned by fire; water cannot wet it, nor can the wind dry it. ... It is everlasting and infinite, standing on the motionless foundation of eternity."[54] Krishna provides us a powerful metaphor for what it means to truly be present in each moment or in the now. It is to rest in this Higher Self, to stand "on the motionless foundation of eternity."

In the Old Testament, God describes himself, and so the Higher Self of each and every one of us, in a similar way. This is evident in the following dialogue that takes place between Moses and God, when he is given the task to free the Israelites:

> And Moses said unto God, Behold, when I come unto the children of Israel, and shall say unto them, The God of your fathers hath sent me unto you; and they shall say to me, What is his name? What shall I say unto them? And God said unto Moses, I AM THAT I AM … Thus shalt thou say unto the children of Israel, I AM hath sent me unto you.[55]

Normally, when we are asked to introduce ourselves to a group of people, we may say, "My name is such and such" or "I am so and so." To introduce oneself as, "I AM THAT I AM," is to say that "I AM the essence of all things named and unnamed. I don't need to be named, for all names are in my name, and I AM in all names."

God is reminding Moses and all of humanity through this message that God is the deeper aspect of life, of being-ness, of consciousness. Therefore, his presence is always with us. The same is also acknowledged in the following verses from the Old Testament:

> As I was with Moses, so I will be with you; I will never leave you nor forsake you. … the Lord your God will be with you

---

[54] Easwaran, *Gita*, 2:23-24.

[55] Exodus 3:13-14 (ASV).

wherever you go;[56]

My Presence will go with you, and I will give you rest;[57]

Where can I go from your Spirit? Where can I flee from your presence? If I go up to the heavens, you are there; if I make my bed in the depths, you are there.[58]

When we remain in this presence, in our Higher Self, in the spirit of God, life bears eternal fruit, and we rise above the suffering of the world. Jesus, speaking from that spirit in his heart, tells his disciples: "Remain in me, as I also remain in you. No branch can bear fruit by itself; it must remain in the vine. Neither can you bear fruit unless you remain in me."[59]

As Jesus teaches us, it is man's choice to remain and be present in his Higher Self versus the ego, in order to bear eternal fruit. It's a difficult task because the ego is always beating the drum of its temporal existence, drowning out the voice of the Higher Self. The ego continuously reflects on who's being nice to us and who's not, from whom we are superior and of whom we are a victim. Choosing presence in God requires a process of detachment, of stillness, of quieting the continuous rambling of the ego. As we are advised in the Old Testament: "Be still, and know that I am God."[60]

This stillness is demonstrated in a beautiful example from the life of Jesus. Jesus visits a village and is hosted by one of his followers, Martha. Mary, Martha's sister, decides to sit at Jesus' feet and be still and present while Martha worries about all the preparations.

---

[56] Joshua 1:5-9 (NIV).

[57] Exodus 33:14 (NIV).

[58] Psalm 139:7-8 (NIV).

[59] John 15:4 (NIV).

[60] Psalm 46:10 (NIV).

Martha complains to Jesus: "Lord, you do care that my sister has left me to do the work all by myself, don't you? Then tell her to help me."

Jesus answers her: "Martha, Martha! You worry and fuss about a lot of things. But there's only one thing you need. Mary has chosen what is better, and it is not to be taken away from her."[61]

That one thing was to be present, to be still, at the feet of the Lord, both within and without.

Living from the Higher Self has immense benefits for our lives. As we let go and let God, our lives start running on autopilot. We feel God pulsating through our being. We experience the deeper joys of life rather than the chaos of running here and there, trying to control everything and everyone and failing at it. We experience less stumbling, falling, crying, blaming, fighting, hating, and fearing, all tact of a self-sustaining ego. We experience more joy, delight, laughter, hope, love, peace, and contentment, all attributes of the life-breathing eternal self.

As God looks out through our being onto the plain of life, everything falls into place. We find clarity, like we have never before. We do more and think less; we achieve more and speak less. Thereafter, no matter how many challenges our life circumstances throw at us, we always remain in bliss, resting in peace. Krishna teaches us: "As rivers flow into the ocean but cannot make the vast ocean overflow, so flow the streams of the sense-world into the sea of peace that is the sage."[62]

This is the peace, the end of suffering, which the great teacher Buddha vied for his entire life. He describes his life journey in the following words:

Just as a lotus, born in the water, grown up in the water,

---

[61] Luke 10:39-42 (ISV).

[62] Easwaran, *Gita*, 2:70.

raises itself above the water and stands there without being polluted by the water – in the same way, ... though I was born in the world and grew up in the world, did I transcend the world; and having transcended the world, I live as one who is not polluted by the world.[63]

Transcending the world is a matter of being in the world while at the same time recognizing that we aren't of the world. Rather, we are of the spirit, the great, eternal spirit, which has always been and will always be, with us, within us. Whenever we rest in that spirit, like the lotus flower, we rise above the illusory darkness and dirt. We shine eternal radiance and light onto life. Resting in the presence of God, we breathe and live eternal bliss.

---

[63] Mitchell, *Buddha*, 63.

JOURNEY OF PRESENCE IN GOD
STAGE 2: PREPARE

Let go of all desires to control your life
and the lives of others.
Letting go starts the process of letting God.

Voice of Man

Dear God, why is my life so crazy? I'm so exhausted, mentally, spiritually, emotionally, and physically. You have given me life, but you haven't given me enough time to live. Everywhere, the clock is ticking, deadlines are looming, failures are upon me, and I'm drowning, fighting a storm. I'm always running: running to school, running to work, running home after work, running after my family, running while I eat, running while I shower, running when I attend prayers, running even when I'm supposed to have fun, and running even in my sleep, dreaming of things undone and fears unresolved. Even though I have been running so much, the doctors keep telling me that my physical health has never been worse. I'm taking medications for cholesterol, diabetes, blood pressure, anxiety, and pain killers every day. Even to sleep, I need medication.

Dear God, what has happened to me? I remember being a child who was always joyful and happy for no reason. I remember being free, completely free. I remember being free from the expectation that I needed to act a certain way or be a certain way to be respected, to be accepted, to be loved, to be "normal." I remember spending hours and hours playing on swings, slides, climbing, jumping, biking, hiking, pretending, imagining, and most of all laughing—laughing until my stomach hurt, laughing until the tears rolled down my cheeks. I remember having adventures everyday with staircases transformed into ships, with floors transformed into oceans, swimming and seeing the world. I remember living out stories,

stories in which I was a super hero, who saved the world every day, beating bad guys and rescuing good guys. In each story, I would have a new super power to rise above the challenges thrown at me. Where are that hero and those powers today to save me from drowning within myself?

Dear God, why is this world so bleak? Every day, I hear of more crimes, more injustices, more wars, and more problems. Suffering is everywhere, so much so, that I'm now becoming immune to it, ignoring it, looking right at it, and not seeing it. But, this immunity has seeped deep in my being, so much so, that I'm unable to see my own suffering. Each night, my soul cries in pain while my body snores; my heart wrestles with restlessness while medications numb me to sleep. No wonder I don't feel happy anymore. I don't think I feel anything anymore. I have become like one of those machines that I use daily to make my coffee or to drive myself to work: just a bunch of gears and buttons, pushed so that I'm well utilized. But, utilized by whom or what, and for what purpose? I feel so empty, empty without purpose, without direction, without life. Please save me from this darkness.

Dear God, I now sit in silence seeking your guidance … My heart stirs as I remember a story I had forgotten:

A village girl became an unwed mother. After intense interrogation, she revealed who the father was: the Zen Master living at the outskirts of the village. The villagers trooped into the Master's house. They rudely disturbed his meditation, denounced him as a hypocrite, and told him to keep the baby. All the Master said was, "Very well. Very well." He picked up the baby and made arrangements with the woman next door to look after it at his expense. His name, of course, was ruined, and his disciples all abandoned him. When this had gone on for a year, the village girl could bear it no longer and confessed that she had lied. The father was the boy next door. The villagers went back to the Master. They bowed profoundly to him, begged for his forgiveness, and requested to take the baby back. All the Master said, as he handed back the child was, "Very well. Very well."[64]

Dear God, it was as if I was in pieces, and this story made me whole again. I finally found the way to complete fulfillment. Time ticked for that Zen Master the same way it ticked for me. But, the way the Master engaged with his life was different from mine. He didn't let himself be carried away, become numb or distributed, by life's problems and sufferings. Instead, he remained whole, in the peace within, and brought that peace to everything he encountered. I realized that it was in my own hands as well, to live from that peace, and bring that peace to life.

Dear God, I have been running after life rather than letting life flow to me and flow through me. I have been striving to make life perfect, and in that struggle for perfection, have forgotten to live. I realize now that to live is to just be, just be within, in the now, in the here. It's to accept whatever life gives you, whether it is a flower or a thorn. In the end, what the senses feel, what the eyes see, and the ears hear are just scenery and sound. It's my mind that has the power to interpret that moment into a flower or a thorn. When my mind is grounded within, in my inner being, in the inner peace, then I can interpret a flower as a flower and a thorn as a flower also.

Dear God, being in the now is about being present in the only aspect of me, which is truly real, which lives and breathes my life every minute, which continues to exist beyond death: YOU. Being in your presence allows your light to shine into my life. It makes my life secure and stable. When a car is being driven, there are shock absorbers between the shell and the wheels of the car. As the car drives over rocky terrain, the wheels register the bumps. But if the shock absorbers are

---

[64] Adapted from Anthony De Mello, "Very Well, Very Well," in *The Song of the Bird*, 2nd ed. (Anand, India: Gujarat Sahitya Prakash, 1982), 116-117.

strong, the shell of the car won't feel the bumps. Similarly, as the car of my life rides over rocky terrain, the physical senses register the bumps. The stronger is my presence in you, the stronger are my shock absorbers. Then, less of those bumps will be felt by my mind, felt by the shell of my life. Consequently, the smoother my ride of life will become.

Dear God, I finally understand what the new age movement means when it says, "Let go and let God." Today, I choose to practice this wisdom in all areas of my life. I stop depending on people and circumstances outside of myself to make me happy. I choose happiness in you. Through you, I give happiness to all and experience happiness in all.

JOURNEY OF PRESENCE IN GOD
STAGE 3: ARRIVE

Feel the infinite power of God
pulsating through your being.
Put all trust in that power,
for it pulsates through all of life.

Voice of God

A faithful man once lived in a place that was overwhelmed by a flood. He climbed to the top of his house and prayed to God to save him. A boat came by, and the driver wanted to help the man. "No, go ahead," he said, "I'm waiting for God." A rescue ship came by, and the captain asked him to come aboard. The man replied, "No, go ahead, I'm waiting for God." Finally a helicopter came by, and the pilot asked him to grab a rope and climb up. "No, go ahead, I'm waiting for God," repeated the faithful man. The flood overtook the man, and he died. In the spiritual realm, the man went up to God and asked him: "I believed in you all my life. Yet, when I needed you the most, you didn't come to my help?" God replied: "I sent a boat first, but you denied it. I sent a rescue ship, next, and you refused it. Finally I sent a helicopter, and even that you rejected. What else could I have done for you, my son?"[65]

All of life is pulsating in my being. Hence, all of life is a platform from which you can access me and I can reach out to you. But some are only looking for me to show up in a specific form. They call on me, but when I make myself apparent to them, they look past me as if they are looking and waiting for something or someone else. They have separated me from the

---

[65] Adapted from "What more do you expect?," johnabisaab.com, February 7, 2015, accessed August 10, 2015,
http://johnabisaab.com/2015/02/07/what-more-do-you-expect/.

rest of life. They miss seeing me even when I am in front of them. They believe I live in a far place, away from their daily life and existence. On the contrary, every day, every moment, I walk with you, watch over you, and take care of you, like a mother watching over her child. I protect you, help and support you, like that mother. When you face difficulties, I am there to comfort you. When you feel troubled, I send you my wisdom and signs to know that all will be well, that this too shall pass. But, it's only a rare few who see me ever present.

I am always there with you, working for you. I listen to every single prayer that's ever said in my name. I answer every single prayer that's ever requested from any of my children. But, many times, you believe that I don't hear you or that I choose not to respond to you. That perhaps you have asked for too much or asked for something I can't give you. In truth, I am not limited by the number nor by the complexity of the prayers that you ask; rather, I am limited by your perception of my ability to come to your help. My help is never far away from you. You need to have complete faith and trust in me. Once my help arrives, you also need to have eyes grounded in your inner being to recognize it.

You often say: "Lord, I believe in you, I completely trust you, and I have prayed to you, but here I am waiting still waiting for my prayers to be answered." If you truly believe in your Lord, if you truly trust your Lord, you wouldn't be testing whether that belief and trust is validating itself. It's as if you give some money to your brother as a loan. He returns the money in an envelope and leaves. The minute he leaves, you open the envelope and start counting. "Did he really give me what he owed me?" If you truly believe and trust your brother, you wouldn't have the need to open the envelope, especially the minute he leaves. If you truly trust me, you wouldn't have the need to ask as soon as a prayer ends, "Is it here yet?" Instead you would say: "I know that you have heard me, Lord, and I know that you have responded. I just have to ready myself to receive it in the perfect form, at the perfect place, and the perfect time."

Readying yourself to receive my blessings is about being in the now and feeling my presence within your being. It's one thing to see me alive outside of you in every expression of life's existence; it's another to see me living, breathing, and witnessing your life as your own presence. The latter is my aspiration for you in your spiritual development. Once you are able to connect with me from within yourself, all of life changes. Thereafter, I not only influence you from the outside, I also shape and respond to that influence from within.

Consequently, when the boat or the ship or the helicopter arrives, you know without a doubt in your heart, in the now, that this is the answer to your prayer. After a while, you don't even pray; you just intend from my presence in the now, and manifestation follows. Many of my messengers performed miracles in this way. It's a powerful way to live, completely present in one's source. It's to witness and live life in every moment from the heart and mind of that source.

When you are present in me, you experience the fullness of life. You live complete love, joy, and peace every moment. Every breath you breathe, every word you speak, and every move you make, becomes a prayer. Nothing in life upsets you, gets you down, worries or stresses you. You are completely still and content, even in the middle of a storm. You are at peace even when the water reaches your feet, and you start to drown. What happens if you add sweetness to sugar? What happens if you add brightness to light? What happens if you add wetness to water? What happens if you add coolness to ice? Nothing happens. If all of life is God, and if the one living life is present in God, even in a storm, God is added to God, and there's nothing more there—but God.

I love you, and I am always present in you, my child. Hold my hand as I lead you untouched, unharmed, pure, and perfect through life. Find me WITH you, THROUGH you, IN you, and find yourself reflected in the mirror of life: ALL life, MY life, ONE life.

JOURNEY OF PRESENCE IN GOD
STAGE 4: EXPERIENCE

Experience God looking out at
all of life through your being-ness.
In that moment, you cease to exist
with only God as present.

Voice of Gautama Buddha
(Gautama the Awakened One)[66]

I lay there, completely depleted of my life energy. I was reduced to a light frame of bones: my ribs sticking out, the light of my eyes barely visible in the well of my eye sockets, and my skin all shriveled up as a plant not given water or sunlight. I was a sight of utter poverty and denial of the material world. In the goal of ending suffering and finding enlightenment, I had suffered more than anyone else could have ever imagined. My suffering was made worse through my knowing of what I was denying myself. It's one thing to be born into poverty, another to be born into riches, and pursue renunciation of the world.

"Is this really the path to spiritual enlightenment?" This thought from my inner being struck me like an arrow. I recognized that I had fallen prey to what I was striving to avoid. In my struggle to starve myself of the pleasures of the senses, I had starved myself also of the joys of living and being. My ego, which had initially tempted me with the pleasures of the world and had failed, had tempted me with the denial of the world and had succeeded. Instead of clinging to cravings for material enrichment, I was clinging to cravings for spiritual enlightenment. Either way, I was still a prisoner, suffering at

---

[66] See Mitchell, *Buddha*, 37-40, and Sherab Kohn, *A Life of the Buddha*, Rev. ed. (Boston, MA: Shambhala Publications, 2009), 27-29, to read more about "The Quest For Enlightenment" of the Buddha.

the hands of my ego—the darkness, and death I called Mara.

I asked my inner being, "If this is not the way, what is the way?" I heard the clear reply:

The way to spiritual enlightenment is the middle way between the two extremes of excessive self-pleasure and self-denial. It is the way of intelligent meditation with focus on purity of heart and life. It is the way that leads to tranquility and peace, to stillness and presence, to a happy state apart from sensual and material desires.

I realized what a fool I had been. I had been suspicious of the joys and happiness of being present in my inner being. Instead, it was the key to enlightenment. When I was a child, it was this presence, this oneness that had given to me my first taste of freedom. It had happened at a harvest festival, which I had attended with my father. I had decided to separate myself from all the commotion and had found a quiet place under a tree. There, I had entered into a state of meditative bliss and presence, which had given me great peace and joy. I, now, knew that this was the true way to enlightenment and vision. Rather than deny my being, I had to embrace it and penetrate it deeper and deeper until I had reached the state of ultimate extinction, ultimate transcendence, and ultimate bliss.

I reconnected with my heart and let it guide my renewed effort for enlightenment. I first strived to recover my physical health. Seeing me eat and drink like before, the friends who had joined me in the search for enlightenment abandoned me. They thought I had become attached to the world. Little did they know that I was finally living from my spirit. I meditated with one-pointed concentration to develop my presence in the spirit within and experience the bliss of its presence. As I navigated each day, I carried that spirit with me and let it guide and sustain my every thought, word, and deed.

It was the morning of my thirty-fifth birthday. The spirit evoked in me the thought that today was the day that I had been waiting for my entire life. I searched for an external sign that would make this apparent to me. The sign appeared as I was meditating under a banyan tree. A rich lady carrying milk rice pudding in an expensive bowl approached me. She bowed respectfully and offered in my hands the pudding. She told me her story.

Her name was Sujata. She had prayed for a good husband and a son to the god of that tree. She had promised an offering if her wishes would come true. Today, both her wishes had come true, and she was fulfilling her promise. I blessed her for her offering and went to a nearby river to wash up and eat the pudding. It was a gift of love, and it rejuvenated me completely.

As I returned to the forest, I wondered where I could sit and meditate on this auspicious day. Suddenly, I ran into a grass cutter. He insisted that I take some of his sweet scented grass to use as a seat for my meditation. This was a second sign from my inner being. After six years of seeking, the universe was finally paving the way for my enlightenment. I took the grass and continued my search for a good place to meditate. I felt my entire being halt in front of a tree. The tree radiated a glow I had never seen on any other tree before. I knew immediately that this was the place where I would find enlightenment. This was also the third sign.

I placed the soft scented grass under the tree and sat down to meditate. Nourished by the milk rice pudding, nurtured by the padding of the soft grass under me, shaded under the leaves and branches of the blessed tree, and encouraged and empowered by the signs that I had been given, I decided to meditate until complete enlightenment was found. I slowly let go of all attachments to my temporal self and being. I ascended slowly into deeper and deeper states of inner bliss and transcendence. I knew that the goal of my life was about to be accomplished. The temporary state of presence and stillness that I often experienced would become permanent. My life would be still in every way. I would live completely from and in my eternal nature, my awakened inner being.

JOURNEY OF PRESENCE IN GOD
STAGE 5: RELIVE

O God, I rest in you completely free from all bonds.
Make this state of rest in you the center
of all activity in my life.

Voice of Shafeen

It was the summer of 2007. I was away from home for three weeks at the Second Episode of an International Residential Program in London, United Kingdom. As sponsored by my religious community, I was being trained to become an *Al-Waez*, a faith-based speaker. After completing the training, I would be certified to complete faith-based talks on a volunteer basis at our community's places of worship in the United States and abroad. During the training, I received a message from my employer in the U.S. It was urgent that they speak to me. After my classes were done one evening, I called the VP at my company. It was still the work day there due to the time difference.

"Shafeen, I have some bad news for you," the VP started. "We are downsizing significantly and you have been identified as one of those who is being let go." As I heard the VP say these words, I noticed that there were no feelings of anger or frustration or worry in my heart. I thanked her for letting me know and received additional details about when the separation would formally occur. As I hung up the call, I wondered why I didn't feel stressed. If something like this would have happened a year ago, I would have been devastated. As I reflected further, I realized what was holding me still that moment.

The year between the summer of 2006 and the summer of 2007 had been the most crazy, as well as the most expansive, year of my life. I was working full-time as a Technology Manager at a growing healthcare company, while attending one of the most competitive part-time MBA programs in the nation. I was a national and local trainer of religious education teachers in the U.S. I was working on my certification to become a faith-based speaker, a program that required research and assignments similar to a PhD. but squeezed in a year's time. I was teaching religious education to tenth and eleventh graders at our place of worship. I was a team lead for Uniformed Volunteers at my place of worship managing the upkeep of our center on specific assigned days of the week. But the most demanding and expansive duty of all, I, with three others, was a custodian of our place of worship, including practice of faith and prayers between 4:00 a.m. and 6:00 a.m. every single morning.

Though life was extremely difficult, physically, mentally, and emotionally, I always felt a sense of peace and stability underlying my life. The source of that peace was the hour between 4:00 a.m. and 5:00 a.m. that I spent in meditation at our place of worship. This hour was intended for all attendees to individually search for divine light within themselves while physically residing in complete darkness and silence. I used that hour to connect deeper with my inner being, with my Lord, and the peace that emanated from him. This hour sustained me through the rest of the twenty-three hours every day.

There were days when I would be standing giving my duty as a Uniformed Volunteer. I would feel so tired that I thought I would fall at any moment. In those moments, I felt a presence—undeniable, irrefutable, and full of strength—which carried me through that moment and every moment. I knew it was the Lord, sustaining me on the outside and sustaining me on the inside, through the presence that I established in him every morning in that hour of meditation.

There were days when I had tests for which I didn't have any time to study. I remember a multiple choice test for a statistics class in which there were twenty questions that required computation. As a High School Valedictorian and a College graduate with Honors, the possibility of failing a test was an extremely foreign situation. For the first time in my life, that possibility seemed very real. I turned to the Lord within and said: "Dear God, I don't know the answers to any of these questions. You take care of this test." Thereafter, I went question by question and marked, randomly, A, B, B, D, C, A... A few days later, when I received the test back, I had gotten two questions wrong and a 90 percentile on the test. Though I was immensely grateful, a part of me completely expected the result. I knew that the Lord would take care of this test.

At the place of worship, at 5:00 a.m., it was my duty to announce the end of meditation every day through the recitation of a prayer. The prayer was the cue for all lights in the prayer hall to be opened. There was a hidden clock that always showed the time so I knew when I was supposed to end the meditation. However, there were many days when I was so tired that I fell asleep while meditating. Yet, not once in the period of that year did I miss doing that duty. On more than one occasion, at 4:59 a.m., my eyes would open. My Lord residing in me was awake, while I was asleep, keeping an eye on the clock. He would wake me up before the prayer was due.

The biggest miracle that came in my life during that year was my wife. Before that year, every relationship that I had engaged in, in search of a significant other, had not ended well. I had brought an incomplete, insecure, and unworthy self to each relationship. For the first time in my life, that year, I felt complete due to my presence in the eternal. In that state of being, one evening, I told the Lord: "Lord if you bring someone into my life as a significant other tomorrow, I'll pursue that relationship with all my heart and soul. I will fulfill that relationship no matter what challenges or barriers I encounter on the way."

The next day, I received an email from a family friend who I barely saw once a year telling me that there was a perfect girl that I had to meet. At the same time, she had reached out to my wife-to-be about a perfect guy that she had to meet. I wanted to reassure myself that this was coming into my life from the Lord. To test this, I tried pushing away the opportunity, making the excuse that I was too busy to engage in a relationship. Unbeknownst to me, my wife-to-be was making the same excuse with the family friend. Yet, driven by the Lord, the family friend would take no excuses. She was adamant that the two of us had to meet and made sure that we had our first conversation. One conversation led to another and another and a relationship blossomed that year where the other part of my soul came into my life. She understood me better than anyone in my life. I was able to share my life with her including my special relationship with the Lord.

These are some of the many miracles that occurred that year in the Lord's presence. There was never a moment when I was in despair. The Lord always directed me to "what can be done right now about this situation." He always focused me on the solution rather than the problem. He always reminded me that all was well, all is well, and all will be well. He taught me that it was not the life of the body but rather the life of the soul that was eternal. I followed his lead, and found his hand at every turn and every corner. As long as I remembered to turn to him, he made himself evident in small and big ways to show his presence in my life.

After finishing the phone call with my VP, I reflected on my upcoming layoff. I pleasantly thought to myself: "Ahh, the Lord is giving me some well-earned rest for quite a busy year. This will allow me to catch up." I thanked the Lord graciously, took his name silently in my heart, and later joined my colleagues at the residential program for dinner.

As I ate dinner, the Lord reminded me to assess where I was. I was sitting at tables with seventy other brothers and sisters from around the world. They represented seventeen different countries, spoke different languages, came from different cultures, and looked completely different from each other. But in each heart, I saw the same Lord living, breathing, talking, laughing, and resting. I was in heaven with a group of people who all felt the Lord in their heart and were there to give their life to him. I felt so privileged and humbled that he had chosen me for this experience. As I reflected on this thought, the Lord corrected me from within. He said: "It's not I who has chosen you, my son, but you who have chosen me. You have chosen me as your place of being, as your place of rest. Witness your life as it unfolds through my eyes as I make it shine brighter than the stars."

I rested in bliss knowing that everything the Lord said would come true. He had led me thus far through the storms, the valleys and the mountains of my life. I was willing to walk in the dark as well as the light knowing that he, and his presence, would accompany me wherever I would go.

JOURNEY OF PRESENCE IN GOD
STAGE 6: CONVERSE

My child, there's no better peace
than in my essential being.
Rest in my peace and find your eternal self.

Voices of Man and God

Man: O God, there are those who face extreme trials and tribulations, who are in constant turmoil, despair or depression, sometimes initiated not by themselves but by external physical or environmental influences. How can the now, the inner being, be experienced by such people?

God: It's true that each human being is at a different point of living. I say a point because all their beliefs, all of their experiences, all of their strengths and weaknesses, boil down to a point of life, a point of living. This point is not a physical point. It's an emotional and mental point, a spiritual point, which reflects their entire being. This point, though arrived at differently by each individual, based on each individual's circumstances, is by nature a point, the geometry of it being the same.

When you map something on a GPS, the address where you start from is a point and the address where you are going is a point. Each starting point and destination point looks different because it has your orientation in it, but at the end of the day, whether you are at the start, or you are at the end, you are at a single location, a single place of being. This is what I mean above. Whoever the human being is, whatever are his circumstances, if he's a fully conscious being (not someone who's completely unaware of his own existence due to a handicapping ailment or mental condition), it's available to him the opportunity to focus on this point. Whether rich or poor, starving or full, this point, this space, this now, is available to him.

Obviously, it's easier for someone who has a full stomach rather than a starving stomach to focus on that point but that doesn't mean it's impossible. Everyone can focus there especially those who are mentally tortured by the ego, by emotional pain, by an imbalance in their thoughts or feelings. For them, this space of now holds the largest rewards of peace and enlightenment. It's like any muscle, like any development, one desires to undertake at a physical level. In order to develop, one must practice. The more one practices being in the now, the better he/she gets at it, the more presence muscle he/she develops. It's not so difficult. It requires recognition of the space and an immersion of the individual into that space. Once immersed, one finds the feeling of completion, the feeling of love, and the feeling of detachment from all. In that space, one feels good and one feels light.

Returning from this space to the condition of life, one brings peace, fullness and contentment to the issue at hand, whether it is an illness or an addiction. Over time, developing this muscle, one may completely be healed of one's issues and ailments. It all depends on one's ability to connect deeper with the now and in that space finding one's true self. That self is completely free, full and unharmed from all the negative occurrences of physical life.

Man: O God, many times we find ourselves at that point of presence, of now. But then we encounter other people who aren't at peace and not present. Because they aren't, they are carrying emotional charge and vibrations of stress and worry. Sometimes, these people are from our own family. How do we stay in the now especially when we are exposed to the vibration of others who may not be present all the time or at all?

God: Let us ask this question another way. What if someone is truly bothered by you in his life? What if he/she comes to you and says: "Can you please change yourself because you are disturbing my quality of life? You are a horrible, mean, hateful person and being near you disgusts me." Wouldn't it hurt for you to hear that from someone you barely know? Now try hearing that from someone you love. Oh, the hurt, the pain. This is the person who's supposed to empower you, to see you in a positive way, and give you the space to grow on your own. This is the person who's supposed to be an example for you. If you are in the dumps, he/she is the supposed to be the light near you that you can learn from, that you can mimic to find your light. You see how different this question sounds when you trade shoes with the person you are talking about?

Everyone who's in your life at this moment is there for a reason. I am not saying that you should put up with abuse, verbal or physical, from anyone. A relationship that destroys you must be ended. You must seek refuge, you must say "no" to that individual and that situation, and find yourself a better place in life. But sometimes, the above question is asked not in reference to someone who's hurtful in your life but rather someone who's difficult. This may be someone who challenges your way of being, for example, your parents, your siblings, your children, and your spouses. In those cases, these people have been put into your life for your growth, for your learning.

When you go to the gym and you sit on a machine, you don't start complaining the minute that you experience resistance from the weights on the machine. You don't say: "What kind of a machine is this that resists me? How dare it do that? Why is it set to make me feel uncomfortable?" You recognize that the machine is there to actually offer you resistance so that you can lift that weight and build muscle. Later, you are able to lift more weight. There's no end to the resistance. As you progress and become stronger, you are able to move the resistance higher and able to lift heavier loads.

In life, it's the same way. As your presence muscle becomes stronger, you are able to deal with even rougher people and circumstances. You treat them as your test to be able to test your muscle, to exercise it, so that it grows. For some reason, people expect that as they turn to a peaceful life, that all of life should turn into peace for them. This doesn't make sense.

When you ask for a promotion at work, your boss doesn't give you less responsibility. On the contrast, more is given to you because you have proven the ability to handle the existing work load. Similarly, when you seek a higher peaceful life, you are given more opportunities to be peaceful, to be present, and to be aware. You are tested for it, by people and circumstances closest to you.

And so yes, you'll fail at it, you'll lose your cool, and you'll go out of the presence and peace. That's okay. It's okay because some days, your body is so tired that you are unable to lift the weight that you are used to and so you take a break from the gym that day. But make sure you go back to the gym after resting. Taking a break doesn't mean quitting completely on building that muscle. It's the same way for being in the now, for being in the moment, for being in God.

In those moments when you face people who emit vibrations of anger, frustrations, and hurt, anchor yourself in my presence within you. You will be able to sustain against if not soothe that vibration. When you are detached from life, from taking anything personally, no matter how much fire and dung anyone throws at you, your clothes remain immaculate. You become an example for those individuals, a mirror in which they see their own bad as well as the potential for good. It may take multiple encounters before they change their ways but you'll grow stronger each time you are able to endure.

You'll also feel more compassion, more empathy, and more love for those individuals, the more you endure. You'll feel the pain in their soul that causes them to act that way. You'll become the channel of my presence for them until they are completely transformed. This is the way many of my teachers transformed the most hurtful of men and women. You'll find many examples from Muhammad to Jesus to Moses to the Buddha. They stood in front of the most humiliating of words and deeds and were able to shine their light to calm the darkness of the other. This takes a lot of spiritual muscle but I see that potential in each of you, just as I saw it in my messengers.

Man: O God, I see myself oscillating always between the presence that you have described, and the worry, the chaos, the frustration, the blame, the past, the future, and everything else that takes my attention away from that presence, from the now. Is it your expectation that we remain in the now 24/7? Is that even possible?

God: My expectation is that you do your best to be in my presence, and through that presence, live your life. You worry about time. Time is negligible. You worry about your performance against some sort of a standard. There's no standard. It's a matter of committing oneself and allowing oneself to enter the grace of God and letting that grace shine forward in one's life. If you try to control this process, you go about it the wrong way. You are trying to break the lock to enter a door that's already open. Remember, the first step is to let go, to let go of the notion of controlling your life. It's only from this place that you can enter my presence. Once within, that presence will flow into your life, not just in a passive manner, but as thought, word and deed. I'll act through you. You'll act from a place of peace, of rest, of light.

You see this when you look at monks who have been practicing peace and awareness for a long time. They may look like they are sweeping the floor but in each motion of the hand, it's as if an entire world is being created. You can feel the presence in their being even in such a simple act. When you operate from that rest, you embody the same presence. Then, even in the most physically crazy circumstances, you'll be on autopilot. You'll absorb nothing of physical worries or frustrations. As you live your life completely free, you'll have a smile on your face, and you'll bring smiles upon the faces of others. This is what I expect from you.

Of course, you won't get there overnight. Of course, this will be a process that will unfold with practice. And of course, you'll falter and lose it. But you'll also find it again. Eventually, you'll become an emissary of my peace. Don't worry about perfection; don't worry about performance. Just focus on giving yourself to the process and practicing it as best as you can. In order to assess your presence in the now, use the current moment as a comparison. Ask the question, "Am I in the now, now?" Having asked that question, and knowing the answer, make a shift towards the now if you aren't there. The more you do this, the more you will sustain this feeling, this way of being, longer and longer. As your presence muscle becomes stronger, this will come naturally to you. You'll become the master and facilitator of your life, of your way of being, every second, every minute, every moment.

JOURNEY OF PRESENCE IN GOD
STAGE 7: REALIZE

I now complete the tasks of my life
with clear presence in God.
I rest in his hands as he does my work.

Voice of Reader

As I return back to my day to day life, I reflect on the following questions to apply lessons from this journey:

* What new insights did I receive through this journey about life and about God?

- What changes will I make in my daily life as a result of these new insights?

- How will these changes help me live a more fulfilled and meaningful life?

Journey of Guidance from God

God as the Giver of direction

'Lord, I'm down here trying to do what's right. I think I'm right. I am here taking a stand for what I believe is right. But Lord, I must confess that I'm weak now, I'm faltering. I'm losing my courage. … The people are looking to me for leadership, and if I stand before them without strength and courage, they too will falter. I am at the end of my powers. I have nothing left. I've come to the point where I can't face it alone.'
It seemed as though I could hear the quiet assurance of an inner voice saying: 'Martin Luther, stand up for righteousness. Stand up for justice. Stand up for truth. And lo, I will be with you. Even until the end of the world.'

— Martin Luther King, Jr., *The Autobiography of Martin Luther King, Jr.*

JOURNEY OF GUIDANCE FROM GOD
STAGE 1: ASPIRE

Turn within to hear the voice of God.
That voice knows and shows the way.

Voice of Shafeen

On a hilly countryside, a man was once running in the dark. He came upon a curve, but didn't see it, and ran off the curve. As he started falling, his arms tried to grab anything to stop the fall. Finally, he was able to grab a hold of some branches and stop. It was so dark that the man couldn't see anything, not even his own hands holding the branches. He wondered how he could get up the hill. It was too steep to climb, and too dark to see above or below. The man started yelling for help, "Anyone there?" He yelled for an hour, but there was no answer. Not knowing any other way, the man turned to God. "God, are you there?" The man heard a voice inside himself. "Yes, son, I am here." He asked, "God, please help me?" The voice said, "Let go of the branches, my son."

The man thought for some time. Then, he started laughing out loud. This is exactly what he expected from God: foolish advice from a God believed by fools. He looked up again and said, "Anyone else there?" Not receiving an answer, the man hung on for dear life, holding tightly to the branches the entire night. When the first rays of sunlight arrived, the man was able to see. To his utmost surprise, he was hanging a few feet above the foot of the hill. He let go of the branches and landed smoothly on the ground. As he walked back to his home, he wondered who the real fool had been that night.[67]

---

[67] Adapted from Jeanette Yates, "The Strength to LET GO..and fall off the CLIFF!," Restore Your Core, December 27, 2012, accessed August 10, 2015, https://restoreyourcore.wordpress.com/2012/12/27/the-strength-to-let-go-and-fall-off-the-cliff/.

Today, we have information available to us at the tip of our fingers. It doesn't take us long to open up a web browser, type out any query, and receive answers within seconds. For some of us, that process is even faster. We may ask Siri, Cortana, or another smart phone voice assistant, the number of calories in our food, the location of the nearest gas station, or the solution to a math problem. There are experts an email or a phone call away, on any subject, for us to find guidance in our personal, professional or spiritual lives. Because we have access to all this information, we have forgotten the need for inspiration. We have forgotten, like the man in the story above, a very dear friend. He has been with us since eternity and will be there until eternity. This friend holds the secrets of our universe for us, if we are so open to receive. He's there to navigate the ship of our lives, guiding and explaining from within, everything that we encounter and experience from without.

In this journey of "Guidance from God," we strive to connect with this voice within each and every one of us. The address of this voice is the heart. It's the place where all intuition comes from, what we may also call our "gut feeling." This is not the physical heart though the physical heart is a reflection of this heart. It's the spiritual heart, the core of our spiritual being. The spirit of God provides the charge for this heart to function. Just as the physical heart pumps blood in the physical body, the spiritual heart pumps life in our spiritual body. It clarifies and purifies our spiritual life and sustains our spiritual connection with God's light and guidance. Accordingly, the best definition of God in this journey is GOD as the Giver Of Direction.

The word *direction* comes from the Latin word *diregere,* which means to "clearly put straight." No matter how lost we may find ourselves to be, God can give us the clarity to put us straight on our path of life. He's the only one who has the fullest view of our lives, from our perspective, and from the perspective of everything and everyone else. Following his guidance, we can be led to ultimate peace and benefit in our lives. Through our lives, then, we can bring that peace into the lives of others. This was the experience of many of God's messengers and teachers: they felt, heard, and saw God in their heart. Having this insight, they received knowledge and guidance to transform their own lives as well as the rest of humanity.

One of the teachers whose life transformed through his heart was Gautama Buddha. He was a prince who had everything that one could ever wish for in his physical life. However, when he was twenty nine years old, he witnessed three signs of human suffering that deeply struck his heart: a man suffering from old age, another sick with disease, and yet another who had succumbed to death. On seeing these signs, his heart evoked *Samvega*, a feeling of "dismay and meaninglessness" caught up in the suffering of the world. Finally, he saw a fourth sign, a monk in yellow robe seeking enlightenment. On seeing this sign, his heart evoked *Pasada*, a feeling of "clarity and confidence." It was this feeling that led Gautama to abandon his luxurious life and pursue a life of a mendicant seeking enlightenment.[68]

Even the concept of *Nirvana* or "extinction," the prime goal of the Buddha's teachings, was arrived at with the idea of making the heart happy. After seeing the four signs, Gautama reflected on the word *Nirvrta* which means both "happy" and "extinguished" as follows:

> Now, When what is extinguished (Nirvrta) is **the heart made happy** (Nirvrta)? … When the fires of greed, hatred, and delusion are extinguished, that is Nirvana! When lust, conceit, false belief, and all the other passions that poison the spirit are extinguished, that is Nirvana![69]

---

[68] Thanissaro Bhikkhu, "Affirming the Truths of the Heart: The Buddhist Teachings on Samvega & Pasada," Access to Insight (Legacy Edition), March 8 2011, accessed August 10, 2015,
http://www.accesstoinsight.org/lib/authors/thanissaro/affirming.html.

[69] Mitchell, *Buddha*, 28 [emphasis mine].

Another teacher whose journey as a messenger of God started through his heart was Muhammad. Muhammad had spiritual inclinations from a very early age. He visited a cave in the mountains near his home, often holding vigils that lasted days and nights. During these vigils, he meditated and contemplated on his own nature and on the nature of life. On one such night, an invisible presence embraced Muhammad and he heard a voice speak to him. It asked him to "Recite." Muhammad asked, "What shall I recite?" This was accompanied with tightness inside Muhammad's chest as if someone was squeezing his heart. The voice continued to ask Muhammad to "recite" and the tightness grew in intensity. Finally, a silence and ease engulfed him and Muhammad felt the first words of the revelation of the Qur'an stamped upon his heart.[70] What Muhammad was asked to recite that night was the message of God, inscribed in the depths of his spiritual heart. God verifies this in the Qur'an when he says addressing Muhammad: "And lo! it is a revelation of the Lord of the Worlds, Which the True Spirit hath brought down **Upon thy heart**, that thou mayst be (one) of the warners."[71]

Another teacher of God who used his heart to find guidance and courage through God was Moses. When Moses was asked by God to be his messenger to the Pharaoh, Moses hesitated, stating that he was slow of tongue. He didn't consider himself eloquent to speak the message of God. In response, God told him: "Who has made man's mouth? Who makes him mute, or deaf, or seeing, or blind? Is it not I, the Lord? Now therefore go, and I will be with your mouth and teach you what you shall speak."[72] In order for the mouth to be

---

[70] Reza Aslan, *No God But God: The Origins, Evolution, and Future of Islam* (London, UK: Arrow Books, 2006), 33-35.

[71] Qur'an 26:192-194 (Pickthall) [emphasis mine].

[72] Exodus 4:11-12 (ESV).

guided, God had to guide Moses' heart. As we are advised in the Old Testament: "A wise man's heart guides his mouth, and his lips promote instruction."[73] Wherever Moses went, God's guidance went with him in his heart, teaching him what to say and do. God guided Moses through all the challenges he faced, not just with the pharaoh, but even after crossing the Red Sea and wondering in the wilderness for forty years. In one of his last sermons to his people before they reach the Promised Land, Moses speaks to this blessing in his own life. He desires that his people, too, can be guided by God, throughout their lives. He says: "The word is very near you; it is in your mouth and in your heart so you may obey it."[74]

Similar to these great teachers, all believers of God have access to his guidance and knowledge in their heart. As we are taught in the Qur'an: "And whosoever believeth in God, He guideth his heart. And God is Knower of all things."[75] Sometimes this guidance makes itself known as a feeling as described above regarding the Buddha. Other times, it reveals itself through words, thoughts or visions as described above regarding Muhammad and Moses. As we recognize and utilize this powerful source of guidance in our lives, like these teachers, we, too, can become a source of inspiration. Every aspect of our life gets illuminated by the light of God, and we start living a God-directed life. There's no place where God is not, so his infinite knowledge and wisdom is able to direct us and help us in every situation and problem. We also feel comforted knowing that we aren't alone in this life. The great power that created the entire universe lies particularly in our hearts to guide our specific life to its perfect destination.

Living such a life, we redefine the role of the intellect in our

---

[73] Proverbs 16:23 (NIV).

[74] Deuteronomy 30:14 (NIV) [emphasis mine].

[75] Qur'an 64:11 (Pickthall).

lives. Instead of being a rational capability that extends from the mind, it becomes a spiritual capability that extends form the heart. It becomes the in-tell-act: the voice of God <u>inside</u> each heart that <u>tells</u> one how to <u>act</u>. Like it did the messengers of God, this intellect guides us, in every situation, in every circumstance, in every moment of time. It brings us both information and inspiration beyond what we could ever know or experience through any external technology or source. It speaks the language of faith and trust, a language more robust and real than any other language in the world.

It was this voice, or "divine sign," as he referred to it, that the great philosopher Socrates, the father of rational thought and discourse, trusted more than life itself. As he was sentenced to death, based on false claims, he told his friends:

> What has happened to me may well be a good thing, and those of us who believe death to be an evil are certainly mistaken. I have convincing proof of this, for it is impossible that my familiar sign did not oppose me if I was not about to do what was right.[76]

Socrates followed his divine sign even to his own end. He believed that only God was wise; hence, true wisdom could only come from God. Any other source of wisdom that man valued, other than God, was worth little, if worth anything at all.[77]

As we reveal this spirit of truth and guidance in our lives, we penetrate deeper into our own essence, and hence into the essence of God. We find a better understanding of the will and being of God, not just within but without. Our hearts become mirrors in which the full glory of God is reflected and perfected. Consequently, our lives bear witness to God; he knows the way, shows the way, and ultimately, is the way.

---

[76] Cooper and Hutchinson, *Plato*, Apology 40b-c.

[77] Cooper and Hutchinson, *Plato*, Apology 23a-b.

JOURNEY OF GUIDANCE FROM GOD
STAGE 2: PREPARE

Turn your inner ear away from your mind
and towards your heart.
Listen for the voice of God.

Voice of Man

Dear God, I have lost my way. I'm sitting in despair, in hopelessness, in grief, in utter dismay. Life has been unkind to me, and I don't know where to go. All that I held precious to me has left me. All that I called mine is no longer mine. I'm broken from the inside. I'm crying inside all the time, unbeknownst to anyone around me. Why has all of this happened to me? What did I do to deserve such a life? I don't know where to go, where to turn, to find my way again.

Dear God, it wasn't always this way. I had a perfect life: perfect job, perfect family, perfect house, perfect finances, perfect health, and perfect faith. Every day, after the kids would fall asleep, I would get my coffee ready and sit down in front of my journal. That was where I would pray except it was more of a conversation than a prayer. I would talk to you about everything: what happened during the day, what everybody was talking about at work, how my eldest did at her piano recital. You were my best friend, the one who knew everything and yet delighted in hearing everything from me over and over again.

Dear God, that was before I became sick, before I got the news that I had to fight for my life. After that, everything changed. Every day, it got harder and harder to live. I witnessed myself getting weaker and weaker. I saw fear on the faces of my kids and family. I had to quit my job. The medical bills kept piling up, and I didn't have enough strength to see any piano recitals or football games. All I could do was to keep striving to hug my kids, to let them know that I was still there for them. But I could see that they didn't want to hug me back. I didn't look like their mom anymore. I didn't act or behave the way I used to anymore. I was a stranger to them.

Dear God, to see my kids look at me as a stranger hurt the most. That hurt more than the sickness ever could. I feel betrayed by you. A friend, who when I needed him the most, has abandoned me. A friend who I trusted the most has broken his promise to me. Why did you allow this sickness to come into my life? Why did you give me good times at all if your intention was to take them away and give me this miserable life?

Dear God, I now sit in silence seeking your guidance ... My heart stirs as I remember a story I had forgotten:

A father and a daughter were trekking through a forest. In the middle of the forest was a rickety rope bridge. When they arrived in front of the bridge, the father said to his daughter: "Dear daughter, as we cross this rickety rope bridge, the bridge may twist and turn, and you may lose your balance. Make sure you hold on to my hand so that you don't fall in the abyss below." Hearing her father, the daughter responded: "Dear father, it's true that as we cross this rickety rope bridge, the bridge may twist and turn, and I may lose my balance. But, dearest father, I have a request: instead of me holding on to your hand, I would much rather prefer that you hold on to mine. It's possible that when the bridge twists and turns, I may let go of your hand. But, you father, I know without a doubt that you'll never let go of mine."[78]

Dear God, it was as if my heart was blocked and this story cleared all the passageways. I realized that there were two versions of the story of my life: one that my mind was telling

---

[78] Adapted from "Hold me Tight Daddy," Wisdom Quotes and Stories, accessed August 10, 2015, http://www.wisdomquotesandstories.com/hold-tight-daddy/.

and the other my heart. The mind was telling me that when my life hit the rickety rope bridge, you were responsible for bringing me to it, that you had chosen my fate for me. Thereafter, when we crossed it, I had held on to your hand, but you had not held on to mine, and so I was falling into the abyss. But my heart was saying the complete opposite. The heart was telling me that when my life hit the rickety rope bridge, that I was responsible for bringing us to it, that I had chosen the best experiences for my soul's development. Then, when we crossed it, you had held on to my hand, but I had not held on to yours. Moreover, my mind was making me think that I was falling when I really wasn't because you were still holding on to my hand.

Dear God, I know now without a doubt that the heart is right. As soon as the problems hit, I had tried to fix them myself. I had not turned to you to guide me through them as I often had in the small issues of my life. I have grown up in an age of self-empowerment, of venerating and praising the power of the mind; so much so, that in my sickness, this belief hindered me from seeking you out when I truly needed you. Instead of calling on you earlier on, I had waited until I couldn't lift the burden anymore. At that point, feeling overwhelmed with my burdens, I had held you responsible for my misfortunes, for not carrying me, for not supporting me.

Dear God, as soon as I tuned into the version of my life being told by my heart, your voice came through clearly, emphatically saying,

DEAR CHILD, I AM HERE. DON'T BE AFRAID. DON'T BE SCARED. YOU ARE NEVER ALONE EVEN WHEN YOU THINK YOU ARE ALONE. I AM ALWAYS WITH YOU, AND I WILL WALK WITH YOU THROUGH EVERY DOOR, EVEN THE ONE THAT LEADS TO DEATH AND BEYOND.

Dear God, I'm so sorry I didn't hear you earlier. Now, I hear you clearly, and I'm ready to walk this bridge of life wherever it takes us. I know that the eternal companion is with me. I need not be afraid, rickety rope bridge or otherwise, because you are always holding my hand. You are always by my side, this bridge, this forest, and beyond.

JOURNEY OF GUIDANCE FROM GOD
STAGE 3: ARRIVE

Ask simple questions of the source within
and note down the given answers.
Practice talking to and hearing from God.

Voice of God

Once, an ant was crawling upon a desk. It came across a piece of paper on which there were some words scribbled. It asked, "Who has written these words?" A voice from within answered: "That hand, which is resting on that table." The ant climbed up the hand but didn't find anyone telling the hand what to do. "Who told the hand what to do?" the ant asked. The same voice answered: "The head told the hand what to do." The ant continued to climb up the arm, shoulder, and neck until it arrived at the top of the head. Again, the ant didn't find any commander there. "Who told the head to tell the hand what to do?" the ant asked. The voice from within explained: "Dear little one, you have reached as far as you can go physically. But, this is only the beginning of the spiritual journey to find that ONE which drives ALL."[79]

You live in a society today that glorifies man's achievements and inventions. But this society forgets the inspiration behind all the innovation. It's a misunderstanding to believe that the human brain is responsible. Scientists are coming closer and closer to discovering, today, that the human brain is nothing more than a super processor. There's a spirit that informs this processor, a program that uses it for its purpose. Many have identified this program as the mind. But even this is not digging far enough. For even the mind, though more sophisticated than

---

[79] Adapted from Jalalu'd-din Rumi, *The Masnavi I Ma'navi of Rumi*, trans. Edward Whinfield (London, UK: Forgotten Books, 2008), 191-192.

the brain, is in the end a tool, an instrument in the hands of the spirit. That spirit is the source of all inspiration. It births all information and innovation. Every single achievement that mankind has ever made has been informed by this spirit. Every single disaster that mankind has ever experienced is the result of losing touch with that spirit. You sometimes refer to this spirit by calling it "vibration" or "energy." You sometimes measure it through quantum fields surrounding and operating within life. This spirit is my eternal, life-giving breath. Thus, I am the commander above all of life, the all-encompassing, the all-knowing.

Every living being has been given the mechanism to communicate with me through my spirit. I am always present in and available to all. I live and witness life through the point of view of an ant, to the point of view of a star, to the point of view of every human being. Each life, even an ant's, is unique. In each expression of my creation, I participate fully. Some of my living beings live moments to days like insects; others, like human beings, live years; and yet others, like galaxies and stars, live billions of years. There's so much beauty and so much growth in all of life. I only wish that you could see what I see while you reside in your physical life.

Your ability to see the truth with my eyes is spiritual. This means that you have to dive within yourself to connect with the part of me that resides in you, as well as in eternity. When you see with my eyes, you are able to see the formless behind the forms, the changeless behind all the variety, the one behind the all. You are able to witness the light of creation that resides in your heart with which I created all of life.

You have been given a tool for this spiritual journey to find the truth. Every human being has an innate voice within his/her heart, which represents my voice. This voice has a singular purpose: to guide you on the path that leads to me, both within and without. Though this voice is available to you, you have to exercise it in order to utilize it, consciously. Unconsciously, this voice talks to you all the time: the hunches that you receive in times of difficulty, as well as times of joy, the thoughts that you have when you have done something wrong and desire to correct it, the reflections you undertake when you evaluate your spiritual progress in life. This voice is fully active in those moments. Even when you have difficulty in solving a technical problem at school or at work, you can consult this voice. This voice has access to all the problems and solutions that have ever been worked. It guides you to the best way to find the solution.

As you develop your faith in me, I develop your ability to recognize and utilize this voice. Every prophet, every messenger, every inspired being who brought my message onto earth, brought it through this voice. They were able to channel my communication for themselves, as well as for the benefit of others. Each of you has this possibility. You are the child of the spirit of God, the carrier of the light and love of God. As the highest of all of creation, you have been gifted with the ability to connect with me and become my voice.

One important aspect of this voice is that it leads you to me while being itself from me. This may confuse some of my children. How can the journey be the same as the destination? It's as if you arrive at a dark house and can't spot the light switch. In order to locate it, you use the help of a flashlight. Once you find the switch and turn on the light, the flashlight is no longer needed. My voice is the flashlight you use to find my light and to turn on that light in your life, especially in darkness. Being away from one's source, one's essential nature, one's purpose, is the darkness. Since the ego is continuously pulling you into the dark, you need the flashlight again and again to find your way back to my light.

Moreover, negative emotions, such as hate, worry, anger, jealousy, greed, and guilt are barriers in this darkness. If you don't use your flashlight to shine light on these barriers, you may stumble and fall and even lose the flashlight for some time. This is why it's important to be vigilant with the flashlight. It's easy to identify these negative emotions and to shine light on them. They don't feel good. On the other hand, love, equanimity, compassion, selflessness, and hope do feel good, are from God and light the way to God. Once you achieve full immersion in my light and reach my eternal essence, the flashlight will no longer be necessary.

Every moment of your life, you can turn within and talk to me. You can ask me any question of your heart's desire. If you listen to your heart in complete submission, you'll hear the answer. This doesn't have to be only the big questions like, "What is the meaning of my life?" It can be the small questions, such as "What should I do in this situation, in this problem?" It can even be as specific and as simple as asking, "Lord, I'm unable to find parking, in this lot. Where should I park now?" The more you use your flashlight, the more comfortable you get using it in the future for small and big questions alike.

I love you, my child, and I am always there for you, shining my light on all of life so you can see where to go and what to avoid. My light and voice guide the way so that you can reach your destination of ultimate peace, ultimate joy, ultimate knowing, and ultimate en-light-enment.

JOURNEY OF GUIDANCE FROM GOD
STAGE 4: EXPERIENCE

Experience the voice of God directing your life
in the passionate and the mundane.
God cares about every aspect of your life.

Voice of Socrates[80]

The jury had reached a verdict. I was being called to hear it. As I walked back to the open halls of the trial, I listened for the divine sign inside of me, the voice inside my heart. It had been a friend to me throughout my life, guiding me, showing me the way to live my life and to better the lives of others. As I listened to my heart, I knew the verdict before it was read. The jury pronounced: "Guilty with the penalty of death by poison."

It had been a good life. The mission that God had given me was coming to an end. The divine sign had not stopped me from leaving my house that morning or coming to trial. It had not told me to avoid my sentence or protest in anyway. I knew, therefore, that what was happening was good and for the good. It gave me great comfort to know that my soul had served God and my people, and now my soul prepared itself to return to its original abode.

The call for this service to God and my people came in my life when my friend Chaerephon visited the Oracle at Delphi. Impressed by the wisdom he had seen me display, Chaerephon asked the oracle: "Is there anyone wiser than Socrates?" The prophetess answered that no man was wiser than I. When Chaerephon shared this with me, it shook the foundation of my being. What did the prophetess mean that I was the wisest? I consulted the voice in my heart, and it told me to see if I could

---

[80] See Cooper and Hutchinson, *Plato*, Apology, Phaedo, and Symposium, to read more about "The Trial and Death" of Socrates.

disprove this by finding at least one person who was wiser. I thought, surely this would be an easy task. This way, I could go back to the oracle and question the prophecy.

I approached a famous politician in Athens who was known for his wisdom. As we conversed, I quickly realized that this man thought himself to be very wise and that others thought him to be very wise, but he didn't demonstrate any real wisdom. Although neither one of us truly knew anything beautiful or good, I was better than him in that he knew nothing but thought he did while I knew nothing nor did I think I knew. Philosophers, poets, artisans, and many others who claimed to be wise crossed my path after this man. Each of them thought himself/herself to be wise and when we began to discuss this wisdom, to find its root, they found themselves conflicted and confounded. The truth was that they had based their perception of wisdom on temporary worldly knowledge instead of divine knowledge. Since their wisdom was not founded on any truth or reality, I was able to unravel it easily through rational discourse.

Something beautiful happened to me as I progressed on this journey. As I dug deeper and deeper into the true nature of wisdom, I realized its source: the principal of the good, that good which emanates from God. Something opened up inside my heart that couldn't be explained, just aspired for. There were times when I would be in a trance for an entire day, lost in my experience of this good. It was as if I was sitting on the sun itself, witnessing its rays brightening the world. I aspired to bring humanity closer to an understanding and experience of this good. Ignorance of the virtues of the good was the reason why people remained in darkness. Once people understood and discovered the good for themselves, they would bring that good into their own lives and the larger society at hand. In this way, they would achieve the best state for their souls and realize what God wanted for us all.

The greatest tool I had in completing my mission from God was the divine voice in my heart. From a very young age, I had many questions and no one to provide me answers. Some of these questions had been asked by other seekers of wisdom that preceded my time. Instead of a teacher from without, this voice from within had guided me to the answers. I even found this voice present in the mundane aspects of my life. It would guide me on whether or not to attend a gathering, to which I had been invited, or to address a question that I had been asked, or to pursue my daily routine. It would interject throughout my life.

Even within an argument, this voice would take over and facilitate the discourse on my behalf. I would stand witness as it would deconstruct the material knowledge that many claimed to be true wisdom. I was astounded by this divine sign's wisdom, the source of it being God's goodness shining within my heart. This is why I truly knew that I knew nothing. The only one worthy of wisdom was God.

As the time drew near to take the poison, I said goodbye to my family and friends. All were weeping for my upcoming demise. I, on the other hand, was very excited to have fulfilled my calling in this world. I looked forward to the opportunity to move on to the spiritual world. There, I would finally rest in the company of the good, the company of God.

JOURNEY OF GUIDANCE FROM GOD
STAGE 5: RELIVE

*O God, be the voice of truth and
direction in every aspect of my life.
You know the way and you are the way.*

Voice of Shafeen

My friends and I, a group of seven year olds, were kicking around a soccer ball on the streets of Karachi, Pakistan. We were so focused on the exchange that nothing else was visible to us. We were making our way through *Kachi Gali*, the name literally meaning "Unpaved Alley." It was filled with potholes, bicycles, rickshaws, pedestrians, and cart pushers selling fruits and vegetables. Suddenly the ball went flying into an area with which we were unfamiliar. It was the entrance to a slum and some kids that lived there grabbed the ball. As seven year olds, this was the furthest outside of our apartment building we had ever ventured out. The slum kids were smiling at us, holding up the ball as if inviting us to take it from them. They were dressed in old tattered clothes and were barefoot. As we would take a few steps forward, they would take a few steps back into the slums. They were slowly getting us to come after them into the slums.

It was my ball and I really wanted it back. My mind kept saying, "Go get your ball from them." So I continued stepping forward towards the kids and into the slums. My friends, willing to support me, did the same. My life was centered on my toys and a soccer ball didn't come cheap. Suddenly, something happened that I couldn't explain. A voice inside me said "Run!" Intuitively, the direction indicated from within was away from the slums and the ball. This inspired me to also scream, "Run!" As I did, I turned my body in the opposite direction and started running back towards home. My friends turned around and did the same. The kids from the slums chased after us for some time but let us go once we were far beyond their area. Often, I have wondered what could have happened if we had gone after the ball into the slums. That scene often reminds me of the movie "Slumdog Millionaire" and the fate of young kids who drift far away from home.

Some may argue that what I had experienced that day was a "Fight or Flight response." Though a Flight response was eventually executed, a usual "Fight or Flight Response" would require that a living being register a threat, witnessing something frightening or terrifying either mentally or physically.[81] This had not happened. The kids from the slums weren't attacking us in anyway. In fact, it appeared as if they were willing to give back the ball. Hence, I was not threatened by the situation. My sole focus was on getting the ball back. Moreover, at that age, I didn't really understand that this could be a potentially dangerous situation. Finally, I clearly heard a voice inside me say "Run!" This was counter to what my mind was telling me to do that instant which was to go after the ball. Once that voice made itself known, my mind and body followed it without question or doubt. At that point, a Flight response had certainly kicked in but the trigger was not an outside circumstance, it was an inside voice.

There was something special that had begun that day. There was a voice, a guide, a support, a presence within me, in my heart, to protect me, and show me the way. I had noticed this voice before but in a very subtle way. My friends use to love hearing stories and I loved telling them. They would ask me to tell them new stories of Superman and I would break out into one of his adventures. But these adventures were completely original, not something I had seen on the TV or in a comic book. As I reflect back on those stories today, I know that it

---

[81] Kendra Cherry, "What is the Fight-or-Flight Response?," About.com, accessed August 13, 2015, http://psychology.about.com/od/findex/g/fight-or-flight-response.htm.

was the eternal within me that was formulating them. He had access to more information, knowledge, and wisdom, than I had personally experienced, until that point in my life.

Life changed significantly for me as my family immigrated to the United States. We had to start our lives from scratch living as frugally as possible to make ends meet. I had to give away all my toys in Pakistan. To make it up, my dad would take me to the dollar store every month and I would get to pick out some toys. Life was still good because I got to spend a lot of time with my dad. He was having a hard time finding a job and was home more often. When I would come home from school, we would do chores, and go to the park or the library together. However, two years into our move to the United States, my dad passed away after a heart bypass surgery. I was thirteen years old at that time and the event shook the core of my being. It especially enlivened my conscious connection with God, with the guide and the inner voice, within.

My mom was very upset with my dad passing away. She had many questions: "How could God allow this to happen?" "Would he have died if we had not done the heart surgery?" "Are we responsible for his death since we wanted him to get this surgery done?" "Why did he have to go when things were finally getting better for us?" "Why is God making us suffer?" Over and over again, I answered each and every one of her questions. From somewhere the words came and they comforted my mom, at least until she would have the same questions again, which I would also answer.

Before that experience, I had never experienced the death of a family member. I had no source of knowledge, religious or otherwise, about life and death. And yet, the answers that were provided to my mom reflected a clear knowledge and experience of what it means to die and what it means to live. For two years after my dad's death, when I was not helping my family, I chose to spend time in solitude. During lunchtime, while my friends played at the playground, I sat at a bench in silence. I chose to connect deeper with my inner self, with the part of me that knew life from a larger perspective.

The capacity grew later in my teenage years. It would be as if I was having a telephone conversation with a friend, except that this friend was God. No one else, not even my family, knew about this. It was a secret within my heart that I had direct access to this super force that ran the universe, and drove my world. However, some things happened due to which I lost my faith in this friend. Specifically, there were some romantic interests I had which this inner friend promised would be fulfilled. When they didn't come true, I stopped believing in the truth of this voice.[82] I stopped having faith. I was a child who was impatient, who was not willing to wait for the perfect time, the perfect place, and the perfect form for my wishes to come true. Years later, as I married my beautiful wife, I knew that God had fulfilled those wishes. It's just that they had not come on my time but rather on his time.

Today, I talk to the Lord throughout the day. I now have a vocabulary for him that stems from my faith: my *Inner Imam*. Many times, I only ask, "Are you there?" and he responds, "Yes, my son, I am here." Sometimes I enter the parking lot for evening prayers at our place of worship and noting that the parking lot is full, I ask the Lord, "Where should I park, Lord?" "Across," the Lord says. I don't fully understand the answer. I drive up to the back entrance to drop off my wife and kids. Before I can drop them off, I see across from that entrance a miraculous spot that's open. Perhaps someone had to leave early and as he left, I arrived. As I park my car, I smile and say, "So that's what you meant Lord when you said, 'Across.'"

Sometimes people feel that they should only approach God when they have something serious to talk about. We imagine God to be like a CEO, whose calendar we need to get on, when we can't work things out for ourselves. When such a

---

[82] In the Relive stage of the "Journey of Purpose through God," I discuss how I found this voice again after losing my faith and connection with it for a while.

circumstance does arise, we don't go to the CEO. We go, instead, to a Manager, who we feel can take our request to the CEO. We believe that the CEO has no interest in us and we have no leverage with him.

This hasn't been my experience of God. He waits for me 24/7 to call upon him, for something as small as a parking spot to as big as a death in the family. No matter when I need him, no matter what I need him for, his first and foremost question to me is, "What can I do for you, my son?"

In my heart, I believe, and know that this is a reality for anyone, who TRULY believes that he/she has this access to God and is willing to engage God in a conversation. He's there for you like he's there for me because he loves all his children the same. You are as precious to him as I am to him as each and every one of us is to him. It's not that we don't have access to him; it's that we don't turn to him or when we do, we don't expect him to answer. And so we continue to believe that he is too busy, too far for us to reach, doesn't care, or doesn't exist at all. Since he has eternity, he continues to wait for the day when his child will finally call upon him like a son or a daughter would call upon a loving and caring father, and simply say, "Dad, are you there?" He would then respond: "Yes, my child, I am here. Always have been, always will be!"

JOURNEY OF GUIDANCE FROM GOD
STAGE 6: CONVERSE

My child, all roads lead to me and are walked by me.
Everywhere you turn, there's the face of God.

Voices of Man and God

Man: O God, how do I know that this dialogue that I'm having with you, this conversation and any conversation that I'm having is not false, not something cooked up in my mind? How do I know that I'm not just talking with myself, suffering from a multiple personality disorder, in which one personality is me and the other personality is God?

God: You don't know. You don't know from a mind perspective, from a proof perspective, and you'll never know. Why? Because, conversing with me is a matter of faith. And faith is not something that you believe because you know; rather, because you believe, because you have faith, therefore you know. It's a source of knowledge not a destination of knowledge. If you have faith in me, my child, then you must believe that I am God; I am your Spiritual Father; I have seen you from the very beginning of your existence as a life, and will see you through the very end, until your complete immersion back within me. So, do you believe that I am real?

Man: O God, I do, with all my heart, all my mind, and all my soul. Nothing is real but you. Everything ELSE is truly a work of imagination: YOUR imagination, and the imagination that you have gifted us.

God: In that case, you already have the answer to your question. You don't need to convince anyone else of whether or not you are talking to God. No one needs to convince anyone else of this. Everyone who believes that they have access to God within them, to the Spiritual Father within them, to Jesus within them, to the Holy Ghost within them, to the source within them, to the light within them, to the Spirit within them, to the soul within them, to any other name by which they call me including angel, spiritual guide, spiritual entity, love intelligence, love beauty, Higher Self, Buddha nature, Inner Imam, if they truly believe that they have access to me within them, then THEY DO. I am as real for them as I am for you. And until they live, not just in this life but in all of LIFE, until they live as a separate being from me, I'll continue to LIVE in them and to be IN them and to remind them of who they are. They are ME and I am THEM. And so of course they speak to me for the core of their being is nothing more than me. You see, this conversation only exists until the dialogue becomes a monologue, until the two voices become one voice, my voice. Then there's no need for guidance because the river has merged into the ocean, the one who's guided has become the guide.

Man: O God, I know we discussed this earlier but can you clarify again, how do we distinguish between the voice of the ego and your voice? I ask because there have been times in my life in which I thought I was talking to you. I was given instructions that I followed or expectations that I believed. When those didn't come true, I lost faith. I stopped believing that you were there to guide me, to show the way, to speak to me.

God: Some people have defined the EGO as an abbreviation meaning EDGING GOD OUT. That definition truly speaks to the situation that you describe above in your question. In that case, your ego was edging me out. What you were hearing was the voice of your ego, guiding you to what it felt was your truth. When that truth didn't withstand the test of time, the faith, upon which your trust in me and your relationship with me depends, was shaken. Consequently, you went away from me for some time. So how could you have known that this was not God?

Ahh, but you see, even that was a part of your journey to God. You expect communication with me like a phone call in which you dial a number and I pick up on the other side. Though this is true, it's true for a believer with lots of faith and lots of practice. I am eternally waiting for you on the other line but not all of you believe this to be true or know where to find me. Often times, your communication with me is like trying to find a radio station without knowing the exact number. It's as if you were told that in Dallas, there's one station on the FM frequency which broadcasts Indian music. So you go scanning station by station on the FM frequency listening to whether what you are hearing is Bollywood music.

Now this would still be a manageable process if you could hear each station clearly. But what if there's noise disturbing the signal: the argument you had with your coworker, the stress about the deadlines, the worry about the next exam, the project due on Friday. I am not done yet. There's one more challenge. That ego, that entity that wants to edge me out, has a vested interest in what's happening. He benefits from you listening to his station so he's broadcasting what seems close to Indian music on each station. You have to listen to each station for some time before you can finally decipher whether that station is it.

This is probably sounding really difficult already. But you forget, you have a lot of time to do this and this happens very quickly within you, much faster than in a car with an actual radio. Also, once you find my voice, once you find the right station, your belief in that station allows you to store the number of that station in memory. Next time, you don't have to scan. However, if you lose your faith in me, or ignore this connection and forget what it's like to talk to me, then you would need to do the scanning again.

You'll identify the right station and recognize that it's me by the guidance provided. It will resonate with the truth of your life. It will feel good in the heart. You will feel that the problem that you brought and the solution that was offered were an exact fit. You get better and better at this the more you practice and the more you believe. Obviously, it helps to have less noise in your life. Obviously, a deeper connection with oneself through meditation, through prayer, through contemplation and reflection, helps. Obviously, doing this regularly, every day, every moment, helps. It becomes natural, so much so, that you hear my voice as if I was physically with you every minute, every second.

Man: O God, I have some confusion regarding the heart and the mind. Earlier, one of the inspirations stated: "Turn your inner ear away from your mind and towards your heart." Why is that? Isn't the mind also a gateway to God? Don't we need both the mind and the heart to live out your truth and to connect with you fully?

God: The answer to this question depends on your understanding of the heart and the mind. There have been many definitions across time and age that have been given for the two. In some cases, the two have been pitted up against each other as enemies, with the mind as the chariot of the ego and the heart as the chariot of the spirit of God. One has been defined as the source of reason and logic, and the other as the source of intuition and instinct. One has been considered the home of thoughts, and the other the central place where all feeling and being takes place.

Though there's truth to this struggle, in an enlightened individual, the heart, the mind, and the body are all aligned. Such a struggle doesn't exist. Within such an individual, the heart, possessing the spirit of God, is the master of the mind; the mind, possessing the ego or the personal identity of the individual, is the master of the body. In alignment, they all reflect the spirit of God and thus are fully guided by me. The imbalance happens when an individual is not grounded in the heart. In that case, he/she operates primarily from the mind and the ego, serving selfish desires and interests.

Turning your inner ear towards the heart is the act of grounding your being into the heart. It's to make the heart the place from which your life is lived. It's submission to my will, to my spirit, that resides in your heart. But this requires inner practice, to develop one's relationship with that spirit and its utility in every aspect of life.

You may have heard the statement that someone has a "black heart." This doesn't literally mean that this person has a black heart because the heart is always filled with my light. What it means is that the person in question has ignored his heart and the spirit within it for so long, that veils of darkness surround his heart. These veils prevent him from being in touch with his true self. Consequently, in his daily life, this person may exhibit a nature of darkness, of emptiness, of being away from his source and acting from that distance in the way he lives his life. He may demonstrate meanness, cruelty, selfishness, and violence. At some point in his life, this person may experience a life tragedy or circumstance that may force him to reflect on his life and question whether his true reality is the darkness in which he has found himself. Then, the right people or circumstances may lead him further towards his heart.

As this person participates in prayer, meditation, contemplation, generosity, appreciation, and compassion, he may reconnect with the spark, the light, which resides in his heart. The light in his heart would shine brighter and illuminate the temple of his soul. This illumination would then penetrate through any veils of darkness that may surround his heart. It would penetrate through the mind into the complete being of the concerned individual. Thereafter, when people come into contact with such a being, they would experience love and light. He would no longer have a "black heart."

I also want to clarify something else. Thoughts or words aren't the only forms of guidance that I provide to you. Many times, I send you feelings in your heart. In times when you feel neglected and unloved, I send you feelings of being cared for, nurtured, and loved. In times when you feel tired and exhausted, I send you feelings of infinite energy and relaxation. In times when you feel afraid and scared, I send you feelings of security and courage. All the time, I am sending you not just thoughts but feelings so that you can ultimately be at peace. Peace sounds like a destination, like an event, but it's really a feeling, a feeling that is experienced in the heart. But if you are not grounded in the heart, you will not register these feelings, this peace.

I watch over you, I think of you, I pray for you. There's not one moment in your life that you are alone. I am with you in your joys. I am with you in your sadness. I am with you as you sleep, as you wake up, as you walk, as you sit, as you talk. I am in every moment that you breathe, that you live. Without me by your side, my promise to you would be unfulfilled, the promise that I'll always be with you. When you go far from me, your heart will let you know. You'll have the feeling of being lost. When you feel this, come find me again. I'll show you the way that leads you back to your heart, to my heart.

JOURNEY OF GUIDANCE FROM GOD
STAGE 7: REALIZE

I now nurture the garden of my life
with clear guidance from God.
He envelops me with light
whether its day or night.

Voice of Reader

As I return back to my day to day life, I reflect on the following questions to apply lessons from this journey:

- What new insights did I receive through this journey about life and about God?

- What changes will I make in my daily life as a result of these new insights?

- How will these changes help me live a more fulfilled and meaningful life?

Journey of Giving of God

God as the Garden of delight

Goodness and all it connotes is not an attribute. Goodness is God. Goodness conceived as apart from his is a lifeless thing. ... All the dry ethics of the world turn to dust because apart from God they are lifeless. Coming from God they come with life in them. They become part of us and ennoble us.

— Mahatma Gandhi, *The Way to God: Selected Writings from Mahatma Gandhi*

JOURNEY OF GIVING OF GOD
STAGE 1: ASPIRE

Give the best of yourself to all.
That good reflects God,
in your life, in all life.

Voice of Shafeen

A door-to-door salesman once visited a house belonging to a mean spirited man. He knocked on the door and patiently waited. The owner saw the salesman from the peephole and yelled from behind the door, "Go away, I'm busy!" The next day, the salesman came to the same door and knocked again. Again, the owner yelled, "Go away, I'm busy!" The next day, the salesman came to the same door and knocked again. This time, the angry owner opened the door and spit on the salesman's face. "What part of 'going away' don't you understand?" he yelled. The owner was seething with rage while the salesman remained completely calm and at peace. The salesman gave the owner a smile and wiped away the spit from his face. Pointing up at the sky, he said: "I better get home before it starts raining. I see there are clouds in the sky and I can already feel the droplets on my face." As the owner watched the salesman walk away from the door, there was only one thought in his mind: "I want to buy whatever he's selling."[83]

It may be inconceivable for us to react in the same manner as the salesman did to someone spitting on our face. The Golden Rule, "Treat others as you would like to be treated," is certainly followed in today's times, but it's followed with an added clause: "and if others don't treat you the same way, treat them the way

---

[83] Adapted from Mitch Albom, *Have a Little Faith: A True Story* (New York, NY: Hyperion Books, 2009), 47.

they are treating you." So, we choose to practice goodness towards others, but if someone treats us badly, we return the same to them and feel justified in doing so. From that place, what we see the salesman demonstrating above seems out of this world. Yet, this is the exact type of behavior that most of the great teachers of God demonstrated throughout their lives, the same people that are respected and revered all over the world. What was the source of their peace, of their love, of their light, of their goodness, especially when faced with situations of war, of hate, of darkness?

In this journey of "Giving of God," we strive to give to life that part of us, which always reflects goodness, just like these teachers did, no matter what the circumstances. In the Old Testament, when the act of creation is described, after every creation is complete, God observes and witnesses that each creation was "good."[84] Some interpret God checking his creation as good as some sort of quality assurance, making sure that the creation was turning out as God intended. This cannot be true for God is omnipotent, holding power over everything, and thus his creation is always as he intends. Rather than doing a quality assurance, God was actually affirming that he could see himself, and therefore "good," in his creation.

In more than one place in the Old Testament, God's essential nature is described as "good," as in the following verse: "O taste and see that the LORD is good: blessed is the man that trusteth in him."[85] Consequently, when God is verifying after each creation that everything is "good," it's as if he's looking into a mirror and saying, "I can see myself in this" or "I can see the likeness of me in this." In the case of mankind, God makes this explicit by saying that he creates man in his own image.[86] Also, after the creation of mankind, it is said:

---

[84] Genesis 1:4-24 (KJV).

[85] Psalm 34:8 (KJV).

[86] Genesis 1:26 (KJV).

"And God saw every thing that He had made, and, behold, it was very good."[87] The words "very good" are used after the creation of mankind because through man, God had provided creation the ability to know its own goodness, its own Godliness.

Hence, good is the first attribute, the first adjective, God uses to define himself and all of his creation that extends from his being including mankind. When we give goodness to life and to all those who partake in life with us, we give God himself. We visualize this good as a garden filled with delightful flowers that emanate the fragrance of the divine. Accordingly, the best definition of God in this journey is GOD as the Garden Of Delight.

One way we can understand the word "delight" is by separating it into its syllables "de" and "light," with "de" meaning "completely." Consequently, the word takes a larger meaning than "pleasure"; it symbolizes "complete light." To become one with God in this journey is to be a flower in the garden of delight bringing God's complete light to whomever one encounters. This garden is filled with a collective community of light givers who eliminate the darkness of the world through their goodness, their light.

According to the great philosopher Socrates, this is the essential purpose of the leaders of each society. First, they need to find the light, what he refers to as the form of the "good". Next, they need to bring that light—knowledge of that "good"— to enlighten others in society.[88] In his teachings, Socrates describes this journey beautifully through the "Allegory of the Cave."

The allegory starts with the visual that there's a community of people living in a dark cave. They are all imprisoned in such

---

[87] Genesis 1:31 (KJV).

[88] Cooper and Hutchinson, *Plato*, Republic 7.517b-c; and Cooper and Hutchinson, *Plato*, Republic 7.519c-7.520e.

a way that all they see and hear are shadows on the back wall of the cave and voices coming from the shadows. The source of the light casting the shadows is a fire lit behind them, which they are unable to see. Since they have lived their entire life in the cave, they associate this to be the only reality.[89]

This is the dilemma of human life today as it was also in the times of Socrates. We have become prisoners of our own limited knowledge. We take material aspects of the worldly life, such as houses, cars, bank accounts, status, fame, and power as reflective of true life and true living. These aspects are mere shadows of real life. They disappear as soon as the little fire, the light of our physical life, extinguishes. Teachers of God across time and age have warned us against succumbing to these shadows of the world. The Buddha teaches us: "Come, look at this world glittering like a royal chariot! Fools are absorbed in it; but the wise refuse even to touch it."[90]

The allegory continues with one of the prisoners being released by a wise teacher. This prisoner is able to see the source of the light of the shadows and realizes it to be nothing more than a temporary fire. After that, he's guided up the cave to the opening where he witnesses the sun itself and realizes the ultimate source of light and life. He sees the grandness of true life, the trees, the sky, the birds, in the light of the sun and realizes how small his definition of reality had been while in the dark cave.[91]

Through a teacher or guidance from our soul, we, too, may find ourselves turned towards the truth that material life is impermanent, illusory, and temporary. There's something more real, more spiritual, that's at stake. Knowing this, we may make our journey to the light, to the good, and, hence, to God. In

---

[89] Cooper and Hutchinson, *Plato*, Republic 7.514a-7.515c.

[90] Mitchell, *Buddha*, 50.

[91] Cooper and Hutchinson, *Plato*, Republic 7.515c-7.516e.

coming to know the goodness of God and expressing that through good deeds, we may come to know our true essence and get in touch with our true happiness. The Buddha teaches us: "'Good deeds' is merely another name for happiness, for what is pleasant, charming, dear, and delightful."[92]

Socrates ends the explanation of the allegory with the responsibility that the freed prisoner now has to go back to the cave. He must not be allowed to remain in the light for himself without caring for the larger society. Instead, he must go back to the darkness and guide, inspire, and lead others in society to the truth and understanding of the light.[93]

Similarly, each and every one of us, once we experience the delight of true goodness, must bring that light and goodness to others. We must now live in the world with the intention to awaken and enlighten those of our brothers and sisters who remain in the dark. This is a choice that the Buddha also made. He could have remained in Nirvana, in enlightenment, for himself but was given the following realization: "There are beings in the world whose sight is but little clouded with the dust of passion. They are perishing through not hearing the Dharma."[94] Accordingly, the Buddha dedicated his life to teaching the *Dharma*, the way to the good, and to ultimate happiness, freedom, and enlightenment.

Living a life grounded in goodness has immense implications for how we respond to the darkness in life. When faced with negativity, rather than getting angry or frustrated, unhappy, or worried, adding darkness to darkness, we would instead respond with light. This light would manifest as loving friendliness, compassion, joy, and equanimity. The Buddha called these the four religious abodes in which an enlightened and diligent

---

[92] Mitchell, *Buddha*, 66.

[93] Cooper and Hutchinson, *Plato*, Republic 7.519c-7.520e.

[94] Mitchell, *Buddha*, 51.

follower of his teachings would forever reside.[95] In order to be rooted in these abodes, we have to be in touch with what "good" feels like in our heart.

Once, someone came to Muhammad to ask how they may know that they are following the right way, the straight path, thus the "good" in their life. Muhammad responded: "Consult your heart. Righteousness is that about which the soul feels at ease and the heart feels tranquil. And wrongdoing is that which wavers in the soul and causes uneasiness in the breast."[96] Therefore, the feeling of tranquility, of peace, of joy, in our heart, leads us to the way of the "good." Any thought, word, or deed, that doesn't make us feel tranquil, at peace, or at joy, is consequently, not the "good," and not from God.

Earlier, we witnessed, in the example of the door-to-door salesman, how he returned light when faced with darkness. We see the same in the life of the great teacher Krishna. Once, Krishna was cursed by a mother whose sons had sided with evil. They had lost their lives in a war in which Krishna aided the good to victory. Instead of returning the darkness with darkness, Krishna replied: "Behold, O Mother! With folded hands, I gladly accept your curse!"[97] Thereafter, he tried to alleviate her grief by explaining to her the temporary nature of life and how each was responsible for his own fate.[98] Hence, he returned her darkness with light.

The great teacher Rama, whose name literally means "divine bliss," suffered immensely in his life. Yet, he always offered goodness and light to all who crossed his path. It was in this spirit that he is called *Maryada Purushottama*, literally the "Perfect

---

[95] Mitchell, *Buddha*, 144-145.

[96] "40 Hadith Nawawi 27," Sunnah.com, accessed August 14, 2015, http://sunnah.com/nawawi40/27.

[97] Vanamali, *Krishna*, EPUB, pt. 3, chap. 28, para. 40.15-17.

[98] Ibid., para. 40.18-19.

Man" or the "Lord of Virtue" in Sanskrit. Speaking from the source of his goodness, from the Garden Of Delight, Rama tells us:

> Anyone who contemplates upon My pure, formless nature, or on Me with qualities and form, becomes of My nature. ... Wherever such a fulfilled seeker goes, he makes the place holy with the mere touch of his sacred feet, just as the sun purifies the earth its atmosphere.[99]

As we contemplate and become one with the goodness of God that resides within us, we, too, become a channel for his light and grace wherever we go. Consequently, we have the opportunity of bringing heaven onto earth, giving good, and therefore, God, to our life, to all life.

---

[99] "Sri Rama Gita Text LX1," Astrojyoti.com, accessed August 15, 2015, http://www.astrojyoti.com/ramagita-24.htm.

JOURNEY OF GIVING OF GOD
STAGE 2: PREPARE

Treat each moment as an opportunity to worship.
Each thought, word, and action is an offering to God.

Voice of Man

Dear God, I'm sorry. I'm so sorry for all the ill will and misdeeds I have brought to life. Please, please, forgive me. I have committed sins after sins. I have lied, stolen, lusted, and envied. I have been prideful, angry, greedy, and lazy. I have harmed others and ultimately harmed my own soul. I'm so afraid, God, so afraid of going to hell, so afraid of being cut off from your mercy. I don't want to burn in the fires of hell for eternity. I don't want to be in a place of confusion and limbo either. I want to be saved, God. Save me, save my soul. I'm willing to do anything, take up any religion, worship and commit myself to you until the end of my days.

Dear God, it's not my fault that I ended up on this path. It's the fault of my parents. They never loved me, God. They called me names all the time, names that made me feel worthless and made me lose my self-respect. So, as I grew up, I became uninhibited in my anger and bitterness. I made sure that everyone whom I came across felt the way I felt. I bullied others, called them names, picked fights with them, and made others feel worthless. It's also the fault of my school teachers. They saw me as a troublemaker and always put me in one sort of detention or another. Not one of them asked me why I acted the way I did in class. Not one of them cared enough to see the pain behind my anger and hate. It's also the fault of this society. Instead of helping me correct my misdeeds, they locked me up in a prison cell away from the rest of the world. Instead of making me feel like a human being, they made me feel like an animal. Once I got out, they put a big red stamp on me. Anytime I found a good job, as soon as the employers discovered my history, I would be asked to leave the premises. What else could I do but steal and take in order to survive?

Dear God, one day I came across your word, and it scared me. I read about the life hereafter and how everything we do here, we have to pay for over there. As I reflect on the life to come, I'm burning up in guilt, fear, and despair. Please save me from the pain and suffering that I have inflicted upon my soul. Forgive me, and help me find my way.

Dear God, I now sit in silence seeking your guidance … My heart stirs as I remember a story I had forgotten:

The mystic Rabia was once seen running in the streets with a torch of fire in one hand and a pitcher of water in the other. The people asked: "Rabia, what do you intend to do with this fire and this water?" Rabia replied: "I wish to burn down heaven with this fire and douse the fires of hell with this water. Then, I can worship my Lord for His sake and His sake alone." Thereafter, she prayed: "O my Lord, if I worship You from fear of Hell, burn me in Hell; and if I worship You from hope of Paradise, exclude me from Paradise. But if I worship You for Your own sake, do not withhold from me Your Eternal Beauty."[100]

Dear God, it was as if I was on death row and this story offered me a full pardon. The fires of hell inside me were doused by the waters of Rabia. I felt light, extremely light, a feeling that I hadn't felt in a long time, perhaps as far ago as before my birth into this world. I also felt as if you had forgiven me, not the type of forgiveness where one says "It's okay" but still holds a grudge or a memory of it. It was complete forgiveness, as if you had wiped the slates clean, as if you had veiled the records of my life. Those parts that were the most unforgivable had become the most invisible.

---

[100] Adapted from James Fadiman and Robert Frager, eds., *Essential Sufism* (Edison, NJ: Castle Books, 1998), 86.

Dear God, the very first instinct in my heart was, "Go do some good." I found the first homeless shelter and became a regular volunteer there. As I served food to the homeless, I looked from my being into their heart and said a special prayer: "you are loved!" As I cleaned up around the tables, I stopped to look into their eyes and ask: "Do you need anything else, brother? Do you need anything else, sister?" Some of them opened up to me and told me the story of their life. I tried to help them if in no other way then solely with my presence.

Dear God, a few years passed by and I was diagnosed with cancer. The doctor told me that I only had a few more months to live. Though for some this would be scary, I was unafraid to die. I knew that a life with you awaited me on the other side. I patiently and joyfully enjoyed the time I had left. Everywhere I went, I made friends and I made people smile; I made them forget their worries and loved and accepted them fully.

Dear God, today, as I lie on my death bed, I see a room full of people. Some of them I have hurt the most in my life. Others are new acquaintances who have only known me recently in my good times. And some of them I don't know at all. Each one is praying for me in his/her own way but saying the same thing over and over again: "you are loved!" As I close my eyes physically, I open my eyes spiritually. I see the Eternal Beauty of your face that Rabia talked about. "Welcome home, my child," you say as I fall into your arms. I let myself be carried high above, to my eternal home, in your love, in your light.

JOURNEY OF GIVING OF GOD
STAGE 3: ARRIVE

Realize that your soul is perfect,
complete of itself, and eternal.
It's the pure light of God.

Voice of God

The great mystic and poet Farid Ud-Din Attar tells the story of a group of birds that set out to find the King of the Birds, the *Simorgh*. Their journey to the *Simorgh* takes them through seven different valleys, each valley offering different barriers and lessons.[101] At the end of the seventh journey, only thirty of the thousands of birds that first set out, survive, and reach the court of the *Simorgh*. Their persistence and love wins through the heart of the king. Hundreds of veils of separation are lifted, each revealing light upon light. As they finally see the *Simorgh*, they are dumbfounded, for it's as if they are looking into a mirror. Each bird sees itself along with the others to be the *Simorgh*. Hence, the *si-morgh* (literally thirty-birds in Farsi) see the *Simorgh*. The many see the one, and the one realizes itself in the many.[102]

This story is your story and my story. It's our story. It's the story of why life exists. It's an eternal story. Each of you has emanated from me. Each of you is returning back to me. The root of every desire you have is this realization of yourself as me, and me as yourself. Each of you follows your own path through the valleys of life to get back to me. When you finally arrive and look behind the veil, you see yourself as a part of the

---

[101] Farid Ud-Din Attar, *The Conference of the Birds*, trans. Afkham Darbandi and Dick Davis (London, UK: Penguin Books, 1984), 15.

[102] Ibid., 214-220.

whole. At the same time, I see myself as the whole of the parts. Some of you may think that to be successful on this journey, you have to break all relations with the world. On the contrary, this story is one of enlightened engagement rather than severe abandonment.

Every aspect of your life—your parents, your siblings, your spouses, your kids, your neighbors, your community, your society—forms the background, the valleys, through which the journey to God and the journey to knowing yourself takes place. Sometimes, you feel that the journey to God resides away from all of life, alone, in a cave, in a mountain, in which you can solely concentrate on your soul. This is a good exercise to develop or regain your connection with your soul. It may even be a regular practice in which you meditate from minutes to hours in solitude. However, this is not intended to be a life time activity. A life lived completely away from others is not alive. If this is what you desired, you didn't need to come to the world at all. The spiritual realm was filled with places to sit and meditate alone. You came to the world to interact with physical life, to interact with other souls experiencing physical input and responding with spiritual output. Through this exercise, you came to refine your soul faster than the spiritual realm would naturally allow.

Every soul you uplift on this journey contributes to the upliftment of your own soul. As Attar teaches us above, all of life is really one, so when you contribute to another's life, you contribute to yourself. In the same way, every soul you denounce, or put down, or are unable to forgive contributes to the deflation of your own soul. Did I not remind you to treat your neighbor as yourself?[103] You and your neighbor are yourself. No other plane of life, of existence, holds a better experience of this truth than the physical world in which you live. You begin your life here with an amnesia, a forgetfulness, of your eternal interconnected nature. As you serve each other

---

[103] Leviticus 19:18 (NIV).

and see the one in each other, you realize your true essence and that amnesia is lifted. Then, when you return back to your source, you carry an enhanced understanding and experience of what it means to be whole.

It's as if a drop is taken out of the ocean and forgets that it's the ocean. As it comes into contact with other drops, it sees its own ocean-ness by recognizing theirs. Later, when it merges back into the ocean, its awareness of its ocean-ness is immensely expanded. It has experienced itself from outside of itself and has come to know itself more than ever before. A drop that has never left the ocean won't have that expansion, for it hasn't grown in its experience of itself from outside itself. Can a mango describe what it tastes like to eat a mango? Can rain describe what it feels like to have raindrops touch one's face? This is why you have decided to come to this world, to have a physical experience of your spiritual essence.

But, just as the opportunity is there for a faster spiritual progression through physical life, the risk is also there for a faster spiritual regression through physical life. The choices you make, the thoughts you think, the feelings you emanate, the words you speak, the actions you manifest, all make a positive or negative impact on your life. When you choose negativity, you commit what's called a sin. But the original root of the word sin is from archery where the arrow misses the center of the target. The center of you is your eternal, perfect, complete, God-nature. Thus, committing a sin is missing that mark. The more marks you miss, the more grows your propensity to miss further, and the further away from the center you grow.

However, this doesn't mean that it will take years or lifetimes for you to come back to the mark. All you need is one pure moment of centeredness: a moment in which you forget all your past miss-takes (misses of the mark) and find your true self. As you keep your focus on your essence, on your goodness, you grow back into your ability to hit the mark. Your life takes a new route towards wholeness, towards goodness, towards godliness.

I love you, my child, and I always see you as complete light and eternal. I don't see the part of you that misses the mark. I only see that which is perfect and complete. When you see as I see, you see your own goodness and the goodness of others. You hit the mark and see others hitting the mark. You give goodness and God to life and receive goodness and God through life.

JOURNEY OF GIVING OF GOD
STAGE 4: EXPERIENCE

Experience the unbounded, unconditional
giving of God through your life.
Your life then reflects the light of God,
in your life, in all life.

Voice of Shri Rama[104]

My brother Lakshman and I had just arrived at the shores of Lake Pampa. My heart was still aching for my dearest wife Sita who had been abducted. I was truly worried for her well-being and desired to rescue her as soon as possible. We had been told by a celestial being that we would find friends who could help us locate my wife at the mountain next to Lake Pampa. We were also told that we had to see an old woman at the base of the mountain before meeting those friends, for this woman had been waiting for our arrival for many, many years.

We spotted a hermitage at the shore of the lake near the base of the mountain and suspected that this was the place where the woman lived. As I neared the hermitage, I felt engulfed in love. It was as if my heart began to expand, and I felt a space around me as if I was walking on air. Through the open door of the hermitage, I saw a very old woman with her eyes fixed on the door. As soon as she saw me, a smile broke out on her face, and she came running at a pace beyond her years. She said in delight: "My Lord, I have been waiting for you. You are finally here. I can't believe my eyes."

She held my hand with such affection as if she was holding

---

[104] See Vanamali, *The Complete Life of Rama: Based on Valmiki's Ramayana and the Earliest Oral Traditions*, Rep. ed. (Rochester, VT: Inner Traditions, 2014), bk. 3, canto VIII, 130-131, to read more about Rama's encounter with Shabari.

the hand of a parent. She literally pulled me inside the hermitage shelter and seated me on the soft grass on the floor. I could see that my brother Lakshman was a little annoyed with the way the woman was treating me. It was very unusual for someone outside of the royal family to have so much comfort and informality with me.

The lady's name was Shabari, and she told me about herself. From a very young age, she had spiritual aspirations and had come to this hermitage to learn and develop. Her teacher was very kind to her even though many of his disciples objected to him taking on a woman disciple, as well as a disciple of a lower class. He disregarded their remarks and instead taught Shabari everything he knew. When the time drew for him to leave this world, he told her that she must continue to wait at the hermitage until the lord would visit her in the form of a human being named Rama. She had been waiting for years every day, cleaning and decorating the hermitage, picking fresh berries from the forest, remembering the Lord every minute.

Suddenly Shabari stood up and disappeared outside as if she had forgotten something. Lakshman turned to me and said: "We are wasting our time here, dear brother. We need to leave right away, so we can continue our search for Sita." Though my mind agreed with my brother, my heart couldn't disagree more. In that moment, to my heart, my most important work was to be there for Shabari. Shabari saw the good in me, the God in me. Ultimately, not only would this good and God serve her, but it would also serve me in getting through the most difficult time in my life.

Shabari came back into the shelter carrying some half-eaten berries. She exclaimed: "Dear Lord, every day since my teacher departed, I picked berries for you from the forest. I took a bite out of each of them to make sure they were sweet and proper for your liking. Here, please have them." As she said this, Shabari innocently took a berry and held it to my mouth. Lakshman almost stood up to block her gesture, but I moved my hand and held him. I ate the berry with joy and smiled at

Shabari for her loved-filled offering. One by one, she offered me berries, and one by one I ate them from her hands. Truly, no one had fed me with the kind of love that Shabari had for me. Lakshman had a look of disgust on his face. He couldn't believe that the king of kings was eating defiled berries from an ordinary woman. At that moment, he was looking at Shabari with his physical eyes. What I saw was a celestial being shining in her pure divine light.

After having spent some time with us, Shabari took our leave and requested my blessing. I blessed her, "May all your desires be fulfilled." I also assured her that she would indeed attain the spiritual level of the highest souls like the teacher whom she served. Shabari happily bowed to us and sat up in a meditative pose and closed her eyes. Within seconds, her physical body was surrounded with celestial flames, and her soul left her body.

We left the hermitage and continued to climb the mountain looking for the help we needed to find my wife Sita. The heartache of separation from my wife was back. However, now it was surrounded by the love and light that I had seen in Shabari and that Shabari had seen in me. Through this light, we would be guided to our good and to the good of all of society. We would rescue my wife and bring an end to the evil behind her abduction.

Voice of Shri Krishna[105]

The great battle of Mahabharata had ended and I had returned home to my kingdom of Dwaraka. One day, I suddenly awoke with the feeling that a dear friend was about to visit. Immediately, I took my stand near the balcony looking for him in the direction of the road to Dwaraka. My wife, Rukmini, was struck by my restless behavior and asked me about the matter. I advised her to prepare the best dishes and the best

---

[105] See Vanamali, *Krishna*, EPUB, pt. 3, chap. 29, to read more about Krishna's encounter with Sudama.

room, for a very dear friend was coming. "There's none so dear to me!" I told her.

Sudama arrived at the palace doors wearing tattered clothes, which were his lot in life. His family was impoverished and his wife had sent him to ask me for help. He himself had not eaten for days. Still, his face glowed with the expectation that he would soon see his Lord and friend. The palace guards, however, wouldn't let him through, thinking him to be a mere beggar. As he turned to leave, I rushed out through the palace doors and ran towards him. I lifted him up in the air as we embraced. I had seen him from the balcony and had rushed to meet him. My wife and maid servants came a few moments later carrying lamps to welcome a most notable guest. They were all taken aback, though, as they saw poor Sudama instead. They only saw his physical form and its utter poverty while I saw his spiritual essence and its utter magnificence.

It was customary for a guest's feet to be washed. A maid servant would usually perform this act but not for Sudama. I took upon this duty myself and washed his feet and applied sandal paste on them. After that, in my excitement, I almost carried him upstairs. I offered him my seat on the swing in the great palace hall. I asked him all the questions that two friends would ask each other after a long separation. Sudama knew that I already knew the answers. But I could see that his heart filled with love receiving my attention. Here was a man who had completely given himself to the eternal within me. He was my most beloved devotee, one who had given up all the comforts of physical life for the blessing of spiritual companionship. This day, I would repay all the struggles that he and his family had to endure on this spiritual path. This day the debt of love would be paid with love, returned manifold.

Sudama had brought me rice flakes as a gift but had hidden the bundle seeing it now as an offering too humble. There was no other gift that I desired more than those rice flakes from my beloved devotee. No matter how much I probed him, he wouldn't make his offering known. Finally, I snatched the bundle from behind him and opened it lovingly. My face showed immense delight upon discovering the rice flakes that I had loved eating as a child. I took a fistful and ate it with much joy. With every bite, my heart returned to Sudama manifold blessings for him as well as his wife and kids.

The next day, when Sudama departed, he had forgotten to ask me for the favor for which his wife had sent him. All I saw in his heart was love and the sadness of having to leave the physical presence of his beloved. He didn't need to ask me for anything for I had gifted him more than what he could ever ask. I blessed him again and again in my heart for both his physical as well as his spiritual life. As he ventured home, I knew that great preparations were being made to welcome one of the richest men of his village. Overnight, his wife and children had been gifted with mansions and enough physical means to support them an entire lifetime if not more. But the physical reward was not for Sudama, it was for his family. For Sudama, I prepared a spiritual reward, a spiritual mansion, in which he would have the companionship of the highest of the high.

JOURNEY OF GIVING OF GOD
STAGE 5: RELIVE

O God, I desire your eyes, your touch, your heart,
and your speech over any other.
Be in every breath that I take in and give to life.

Voice of Shafeen

It was a fall day in September of 1991. I had just arrived in my first class, English, at the Yukon Intermediate School in Hawthorne, California. I was all dressed up with a buttoned shirt, pants, and leather shoes. The rest of the kids were wearing shorts and T-shirts. I felt completely out of place. I was an immigrant to the United States and was unfamiliar with how kids dressed in school. The school I went to in Pakistan required uniforms and I had dressed up very formally, expecting something similar. I was very wrong.

What confused me more than the clothes was the desk in which I seated myself. In Pakistan, I was used to sitting on benches in front of tables, two students per bench. But here, there were individualized desks for each child. There was a small basket under the chair for books and a small wooden square attached in front of the chair to read and write upon. As I sat in the chair, I felt extremely uncomfortable. The feeling of being out of place, that had been there since I had landed in the U.S., hit a new high. In my nervousness, I started rocking the desk involuntarily. Little did I know how light these desks were as mine tipped over with me in it. I fell with the desk and a loud thud was heard throughout the classroom. All the children turned around to see what had happened. All the children pointed at me and started laughing. I heard a voice say: "The foreign kid doesn't even know how to sit."

Truly, I felt embarrassed. That instant, I felt like I had hit rock bottom. For an eleven year old who had just moved to a new school in a new city in a new country, it was the worst mistake he could have ever made. But, the embarrassment came to a jolting stop as God stepped into the classroom. She was a tall, black teacher who represented for me divine grace and order. She spent what seemed like ten minutes scolding the class on its mistreatment of a new student. I was helped to my feet and my desk was lifted so that I could sit back down. Even though I could see that every student in the class was afraid of her, that moment she was my savior. I loved her for what she had done for me. She had stood up for me. Never before had a teacher given me back my self-respect, especially when it was at its lowest.

Thereafter, English class with Ms. Pennington became one of my favorite classes. As I was an immigrant and still didn't have a good handle on English, it was important that I had a good teacher. Ms. Pennington was that teacher. Since the day she saved me, I was very comfortable talking to her and asking her questions. Whenever she asked a question of the class, even if I didn't know the answer, I raised my hand and attempted it. She corrected me if I was wrong but never made me feel like a lesser person for not knowing the correct answer. In that way, I grew under her guidance. No student would ever mess with her even when she had her back to the class. It was as if she was always watching and always aware of what was happening with each student. She had high expectations of each of us and held us accountable for our assignments. Ms. Pennington taught me the value of teaching and uplifting others while embodying inner strength and resilience.

Another class I dearly loved was Mr. Millers'. It was not the topic that I enjoyed so much, for social studies was not really interesting to me, but rather the teacher. Mr. Miller always had fun while teaching. He was always smiling and had a light air around him. He looked like a ray of sunshine and he represented that ray whenever he taught us. He was always calm and never lost his cool regardless of how stressful things became in the classroom. He had a love for plants, many of which were decorated around the classroom. Some students including myself often helped him water his plants after school. My most profound memory of Mr. Miller is of sitting across from him the day after my father's death when I returned to school. I had started crying in the middle of class and he had called me after class and asked me what was wrong. He was the first person, family or otherwise, I talked to about what it meant to not have my father anymore in my life. He just listened to me and was there for me like a friend. He was an example for me of having a positive attitude in life, of having fun in life, remaining calm under pressure, and being there for others when they needed you.

Another teacher who helped me belong in the new culture and surroundings of the U.S. was Ms. Schnebly. I had been very fond of singing and acting in Pakistan. I had performed in a couple of plays and recitals before I left for the U.S. Ms. Schnebly's class, Exploratory, was my opportunity to continue to develop in these areas. She put together a class play based on a "Charlie Chaplin" script that I had acted out in Pakistan. She taught me songs that spoke to the human spirit such as "Yesterday" by the Beatles and "Lift Every Voice and Sing" by the Johnson brothers. Finally, she gave me the chance to be the voice of the United States National Anthem at our school graduation. Ms. Schnebly made me believe that I had a gift that needed to be offered to the world. She nurtured my ability to serve others by using my talents and gifts. She also made me feel like I was important, that I mattered, that I belonged.

Mr. Yoshiyama, the mathematics teacher, helped me develop the ability to face and solve problems. Mr. Mara, the science teacher, challenged me to try new things, such as eating squids. He helped me be more open-minded and adventurous. Each of these teachers was a different ethnic, racial and cultural face of humanity, at least to my immigrant eyes. Yet, each of them carried the essential spirit of love and light in his/her heart, reflecting goodness and Godliness. Through these teachers, I was exposed to the face and grace of God. Through them, I was given the best of humanity and learned to offer the same.

As I ventured into adulthood, I remembered the lessons that my human examples of God and God's goodness had taught me. When people were stressed at work due to looming deadlines, I strived to be the calmness and presence of God. When a friend or coworker would be overcome with worry or sadness, I strived to be the stability and security of God. When I saw someone mistreated, I strived to be the support and strength of God. When someone came to me for help, I strived to be the love and compassion of God. When someone praised me for my accomplishments, I strived to be the integrity and humility of God. When someone looked to me for guidance, I strived to be the knowledge and direction of God. When someone mistreated me, I strived to be the patience and forgiveness of God.

There have been moments in my life where I have clearly been instructed in my heart to give the goodness of God to others. One day, I was walking in Pasadena, California to my car parked in a street garage. My heart asked me to turn onto a street away from the direction of my car. As I did, I came across a family sitting in a van with small kids crying in the back. They seemed very distressed. Something was wrong with the starter of their car and though they were turning the key, the car was not starting. I told them that I could help and got in the front seat and tried starting the car. Miraculously, the car started. Before they could thank me, I was already on my way to the garage where my car was parked.

Another time, while studying at University of Southern California in Los Angeles, I was walking to my car off campus. A man on the side of the street asked me if he could borrow ten cents to buy a taco from the nearby fast food place. I was told in my heart to buy this man a meal. I accompanied him to the fast food place and he chose whichever meal he wanted and I paid for it.

Yet another time, my wife and I missed our flight back home by minutes at the JFK International Airport in New York. We were stranded at the airport for a night. As we went to eat, we saw a distressed woman. I was told in my heart to see if she needed any help. We talked to her and found out that she had been stranded at the airport for over two days. She was on a standby ticket and due to the holidays could not get a confirmed seat on a connecting flight to get home. She had been living at the airport during this time and needed access to a phone to talk to family and friends and make new arrangements. We provided her our cell phone so she could make the necessary calls to get on a confirmed flight. We also gave her renewed hope that things would work out when it looked like she immensely needed it.

Sometimes I come across someone and my heart asks me to say a prayer for them and I do. Other times, I am given specific words of encouragement or advice to convey to them. In such ways, I have strived to give goodness and God to others and return the goodness I have so often received.

I often reflect on the confused immigrant kid who was lying on the floor in his desk in that English class. What had happened to him? His Spiritual Father had raised him from that low to a new high. Many other falls had come in his path of life. There had been many other moments when he was in darkness and felt alone, afraid, confused and lost. But light always prevailed. The Father was always there to nurture and uplift his son from the darkness into the light. And so the son was taught, through his Father's example, to nurture and uplift his brothers and sisters in life: to give God to life, to give God through life.

JOURNEY OF GIVING OF GOD
STAGE 6: CONVERSE

*My child, I see with your eyes, feel with your touch, love
with your heart and talk with your speech.
I am in every breath that you breathe through life
and that you give to life.*

Voices of Man and God

Man: O God, this journey is about giving of good and
through that goodness giving God to others. But what if
someone intends goodness but ends up harming others because
of their lack of knowledge of what's good? Are they truly giving
God in that act? An example is a teacher who desires to
improve the learning in his class. In the class is a disruptive
student. The teacher observes that the other students don't
learn when the disruptive student is in class. So the teacher
ensures that this student spends every day in detention or at the
principal's office. The teacher thinks that he's doing what's
good for the class. But the disruptive student, who's actually
acting out his need for love and attention, feels further rejected
and removed from the norm. This is just one example. Life is
filled with people who think they are doing good when they are
actually causing harm. Are good intentions the sole judge of
what's considered good?

God: I would give you one simple guideline to help you
assess whether something that's intended is actually good. Does
it feel good in the heart to do this act? When something is done
on the basis of the ego, while the adrenaline is at work, it will be
difficult to analyze your feelings. In the example above, as the
teacher sees the student cause yet another disturbance in his
class, his nervous system will increase his heart rate. His blood
pressure will go up, the adrenaline hormone will be released,
and the teacher will experience feelings of anger and frustration.

In that moment, he'll decide to quickly and perhaps rudely take the student out of his class and send him to the principal's office. Now, in this moment, the teacher won't feel good. That would be the simple way of knowing that what he's doing is not good.

What'll feel good to the teacher? Instead of taking the student out of class each time, what if the teacher decided to have a conversation with him? What if, in that conversation, rather than blaming and typecasting the student into a failing, selfish student, instead, the teacher sincerely told the student:

I believe in you. I know all the stuff that I teach you is no big deal for you. You have the capacity to grasp this and more and succeed immensely in your life. So, what's stopping you from doing that? That's what I really want to know. What's stopping you from shining like the star that I know you really are?

Even if the student doesn't respond positively, the teacher's heart will be content. Even if the student doesn't turn around his grades in that class, he'll start turning around his attitude. He'll know that the teacher sincerely cares for him. When the unloved suddenly becomes the recipient of love, he'll truly respect and reciprocate the sentiment. I am not giving you a movie scenario here; I am giving you something that's everyday life if you truly believe in it. You have the power to change situations like this and truly much more by monitoring your heart. When you do what's good, you'll always feel good. When you don't feel good, one of two things may be happening: either the doing is not from your heart (for example you perform a kind act to impress others) or you are actually doing something unkind and acting from your ego.

Some may point out that sometimes listening to the voice of the ego also feels good. For example, you are driving on the road and someone cuts you off. You roll down your window and show them the middle finger. Some may claim that doing that feels good, that taking revenge or returning meanness to someone that truly deserves it feels good. The good that these people are referring to is not really a feeling, it's a thought. It's a validation of the thought of the ego which wants to administer this wrong to right another wrong. When the wrong is done, the ego feels validated and the thought that initiated the deed is validated. But in that moment, if the person turns to their heart, to the feeling in their heart, they'll not feel a feeling aligned with that thought; there would be disharmony, displeasure, and a sense of bitterness. The pain of being cut off wouldn't have disappeared but rather it would have deepened. This person may be saying to himself: "Why does this always happen to me?" "Why does everyone victimize me?" The moment this person steps into his home and the spouse or the kids say or do something disharmonious, he would lose it with his family. Until and unless goodness is cultivated in that heart, the lack of joy, the dissatisfaction, would continue.

Man: O God, sometimes it feels that being good in a world that's bad is detrimental to the safety and security of the human being. Are you suggesting that we let other people push us around, that we let others treat us like doormats? Should we let ourselves and our families be threatened by others? There are examples of Buddhas who left everything for good, for God. Should we assume the same that a life of goodness is a life of complete forsaking of our families and our integrity as well?

God: The Buddha, Jesus, Muhammad, and other masters were so ascended in their feeling and being that they "saw through" their own mistreatment. This is a very powerful ability, to "see through" the negative intentions of others. At the physical level, you only see the one who's trying to harm you. You see the villain. But when you "see through" the villain, you see God seated in the depths of consciousness, even in that villain. Hence, you ask the question: "What happened? If this being that I see in front of me, this being filled with darkness, is in their core God, what happened to this individual for him to be in this state?" The ascended masters, because of

167

their spiritual perception, were able to see then the life circumstances and the mistakes that the person made that led him to this state. Therefore, they didn't blame the individual; they blamed the circumstances and the bad choices. They never took anything that the individuals did towards them, personally.

Some of the masters did push back, they even fought back. However, this was not driven by revenge or anger. Rather, it was their greater calling to fight to preserve life, to preserve light. When they had no other choice but to fight to protect their people, to prevent harm, to prevent destruction of life, then they took their arms, only to bring back the sense of life and light.

One example of such a teacher was Rama. Rama fought a war against the demon Ravana. However, the purpose of the war was to end the cruelty and fear that Ravana had instilled all over the world and to rescue Sita, Rama's wife. Before the war, Rama gave numerous chances for Ravana to return his wife and end his cruelty but Ravana was too prideful to agree. When Ravana was killed, instead of usurping his power and position, Rama gave the kingdom back to one of Ravana's brothers. After rescuing his wife, Rama returned back home to his people and family.[106]

Another example of such a teacher was Muhammad. Muhammad was abused and almost murdered by the people of Mecca because he brought the message of Islam. The message strived to correct the many vices of that society. These included the mistreatment of the poor and the live burial of female infants. Muhammad's followers were tortured and killed. They, along with Muhammad, found refuge in the city of Medina, where they started a new life. But the Meccans still felt threatened and continued to attack and war against them. In order to protect the believers of God, Muhammad gathered an army of ten thousand and marched towards Mecca. Knowing they didn't stand a chance, the Meccans surrendered to

---

[106] Vanamali, *Rama*, bk. 6, canto VII-IX.

Muhammad hoping for mercy. When Muhammad entered the city, he forgave Meccans their past crimes, and granted amnesty to his enemies.[107] This included Hind, the woman who had mutilated the body of Muhammad's beloved uncle and had eaten his uncle's liver, as a sign of her hate and vengeance.[108] As the victor, Muhammad had the right to enslave all Meccans. Instead, he declared all the people of Mecca, including its slaves, to be free.[109]

Goodness is not weakness, it's strength. Goodness doesn't mean that you bow down in weakness in front of adversity. Goodness means that you rise above adversity, that you smile at your enemy and say, "I am stronger than whatever un-good you can ever imagine." My messengers brought this kind of powerful goodness into their life and the lives of others. They were unshakeable, unmovable, like a powerful mountain molded through thousands of years. Someone who's truly good is also like a sturdy tree in a storm. That tree will outlast many, many storms. This is not to say that one who strives for the good doesn't face adversity. But they don't see or feel themselves as doormats in that adversity. Rather they see and feel themselves as the sky under which all of life exists, including their enemies. The ones who truly pursue good are beyond the judgment of anyone else and beyond judging anyone else. They are based completely in themselves as themselves.

At the same time, no one is telling you to forsake your family's security and safety. I expect you to defend and protect your family. The attempt should always be to preserve the life of others. Good can only occur if you have life to give goodness. The teacher Rama chose to give life, hope, and love to all he encountered, even his enemies. But as we discussed

---

[107] Aslan, *No God But God*, 105-106.

[108] Ibid., 78.

[109] Ibid., 106.

earlier, some of his enemies were insane, so lost in darkness, that they couldn't see the light. They were bent on harming Rama, his family, and other innocent people. To protect that life, Rama had to take his bow. Only when there was no other option, did he step in to protect life. Even the brightest of my messengers aren't perfect in their light because the earthly realm doesn't allow for perfection. But you must continuously strive for perfection and for the good.

If one is hurt or victimized in anyway, forgiveness, patience, and gratitude are the way out of the misery that accompanies the anger and hate towards the other party. You can't allow yourself to turn away from the good by succumbing to anger and revenge. You must seek a peaceful way to be. You must find good in your heart and be able to spread that good to others, even to your perceived enemy. After the harm, there's even opportunity to be grateful, to be appreciative, for what remains good in your life, and for the life lessons learned through the tragedy. This is what my highest messengers did. This is what I would do in your physical shoes.

The one who digs someone else's grave is himself standing in a grave. Never forget this. Leave all checks and balances, consequences and punishments to nature and universal laws such as *Karma*. The individual who causes suffering for others causes himself the most suffering. It's as if you were to take a hammer and hit your own foot with it. The pain you feel will be more than the pain your foot feels. The foot will feel the pain of the damage caused, but you'll feel the pain of both the damage as well as the act that caused the damage. Since all humanity is one, when you hurt another, at the soul level, you hurt yourself. Therefore, you feel the pain of the other and the pain of deciding to hurt them, of the sin, of missing the mark.

Since each soul has to account for whatever it does in life, goodness is the best way of being and living.

Man: O God, good and God are taught sometimes very differently by various religions. Sometimes, the act of believing oneself to be better than others or to be more saved than others

170

is part of the process of being good and turning towards God. Do you agree/disagree with this? Do you agree/disagree with the notion of certain religions acting superior to others in goodness, in Godliness?

God: No religion is better than another. I'll repeat this. No religion is better than another. For each individual, there's a unique path to come closer and closer to my essence. Before birth, the individual himself/herself chooses to be born in a certain family and through that birth to be born into a particular religious, cultural and ethnic identity. I don't care to which religion you belong. Let me say this again. I don't care to which religion you belong. I only care whether or not you feel my presence in you. I also only care whether or not you turn to me, like a child would turn, to his father and mother for support, for help, for sustenance. It's only in this way that I am able to help you find a better way of living. The act of believing yourself as better than others doesn't feel good in the heart. Therefore, it fails the test of goodness that I identified earlier.

Good may be taught different ways but it's essentially the same. Good is the feeling of good as one exercises that which is closest to my heart. And my heart loves generosity, helping others, appreciation and gratitude. My heart loves a sense of inner solidity, a sense of peace that's always unshaken, unmoved, undeterred by all of life's circumstances.

This doesn't mean that I am encouraging you to change or leave your religion. You chose the family and the religion you were born into, for your optimum spiritual growth. So try to find closeness to me in the religion in which you were born. Try to find those rituals, those aspects within that religion that speak to you, that speak to your heart. Find those rituals that remind you of me, of your goodness, of your Godliness. The way to me is found in each religion. You just have to seek it. Yes, some people in the religion may not see it this way but you don't have to compare yourself and your religiosity with their religiosity, even if they do. Remember the rule of feeling good. Does it feel good to look down upon others even for their expression of religious superiority? Isn't looking down upon others, or judging others, or blaming others for taking spirituality out of religion, itself, an act of superiority? In that case, what separates you from the problem that you feel exists in all religions? Aren't you also, then, part of the same problem?

Rather than pointing out the problem today with religions, become the solution within your religious community. Become the example of love and light, like the messengers were who are considered founders of each religion. Also, become the example of complete acceptance and complete detachment that the messengers were. Love those who judge you in your religious community. Love those who act with contempt or act with a ritually based and spiritually lacking religiosity. Remember, when you come to my house, whether it is a church, a mosque, a temple, or a synagogue, you are coming to meet me. This may not be apparent in the midst of all the rituals, all the layers, which have been created between you and me. But if you see beyond those layers, you'll see me. If you also "see through" the layers, you'll again see me. This way, each ritual will become spi-ritual, each a way of engaging deeper with me and coming closer to my eternal essence.

JOURNEY OF GIVING OF GOD
STAGE 7: REALIZE

I now enhance the tapestry of my life
with clear giving of God.
He paints my thoughts and deeds
to create a beautiful piece of living art.

Voice of Reader

As I return back to my day to day life, I reflect on the following questions to apply lessons from this journey:

- What new insights did I receive through this journey about life and about God?

- What changes will I make in my daily life as a result of these new insights?

- How will these changes help me live a more fulfilled and meaningful life?

Journey of
Love for God

God as the
<u>G</u>round <u>of</u> <u>d</u>evotion

Love is the only way to grasp another human
being in the innermost core of his personality. No
one can become fully aware of the very essence of
another human being unless he loves him. By his
love he is enabled to see the essential traits and
features in the beloved person; and even more, he
sees that which is potential in him, which is not
yet actualized but yet ought to be actualized.

— Victor E. Frankl, *Man's Search for Meaning*

175

JOURNEY OF LOVE FOR GOD
STAGE 1: ASPIRE

Love all ways to live in the heart of God.
God's heart loves all, friend and foe.

Voice of Shafeen

Once, a poor farmer came to a saint with a request: "O saint, I wish to know God. I wish to experience him. But I know nothing of God. I know nothing of Truth. They tell me I should meditate on God. I have tried and failed for I don't know what God looks like. Please tell me, what should I do?" The saint asked him, "What do you love the most in your life?" The farmer answered, "My pet goat." The saint replied, "Go home and meditate on your goat." The man went home, prepared a place for his meditation, closed his eyes, and began to think about his goat – its eyes, its horns, and its tail. Every day that he meditated on his goat, he became happier and happier. One day, in his meditation, he saw light, within and without. That day, he had finally known and experienced God, in and through none other, than his pet goat.[110]

What is love? If we analyze our experience of love for another being in our life, we may come to define love as "paying attention to the good in another." We hear this in the way partners describe what they love about one another: "I love the way she smiles" or "I love the way he sweeps me off my feet." We also hear this in the way parents and children describe each other: "I love how joyful my daughter is as she sings and plays throughout the house" or "I love that my mom and dad are always there for me." Since the source of good in

---

[110] Adapted from Gurumayi Chidvilasananda, *Kindle My Heart: A Collection Of Talks by Gurumayi Chidvilasananda* (South Fallsburg, NY: SYDA Foundation, 1989), 71.

all beings is the spirit of God, to truly love another is to see that spirit in that person or life form. This is what the farmer sees in the story above when he meditates on his goat. It's through this seeing, through this love, that the farmer realizes God.

In this journey of "Love for God," we strive to become like the farmer, to love and pay attention to God within all of life. At the surface, this seems like a simple concept, but it's a very difficult undertaking. We live in a world today in which we are taught from a very young age to see the fault in others; instead of paying attention to what's good, we pay attention to what's bad in others. As many spiritual masters have taught, whatever we pay attention to, we manifest in our lives. As we observe and point out the hate, ignorance, selfishness, and arrogance in others, we become more hateful, ignorant, selfish and arrogant ourselves. In order to see the good in others, we need to ground ourselves into that aspect of our life, which is pure light, pure joy, pure hope, and pure love. That foundation in this journey is GOD, best defined as the Ground Of Devotion.

One of the most succinct and powerful definitions of God in the teachings of God's teachers is that "God is Love."[111] When we live from the spirit of God, we can't help but love, and so see the good in others, for we see beyond the veils of darkness that are ordinarily seen into the depths of light. As we see the good in others, we become the same and give the best of ourselves to all of life. It's in this light that we define God in this journey as the Ground of Devotion, the source of love, thus, the seeing and giving of love to all life. This love is the reason that life was created. This love is also the virtue most exemplified by the teachers of God themselves.

Before creation began, before anything existed, God loved to be known and experienced. The only way for God to do so was to be able to see and experience himself from a perspective outside of himself. This was the inspiration for all of creation. In a tradition that many Muslim mystics attribute directly to

---

[111] 1 John 4:8 (NIV).

178

God, God tells us: "I was a hidden treasure and I **loved to be known**; so I created the creatures and made Myself known to them; so they knew Me."[112]

One of the creatures that God created was man in whom God breathed his own spirit. As God instructs the angels in the Qur'an: "So, when I have made him and have breathed into him of My spirit, do ye fall down, prostrating yourselves unto him. So the angels fell prostrate, all of them together."[113] Because God breathed his spirit into man, man was raised above all of the rest of creation, including the angels in his knowledge of God. This is why the angels prostrated unto man. But, man was also made to forget this knowledge and awareness of his true identity as God's spirit. As God says in the Qur'an: "Surely We created man of the best stature, then we reduced him to the lowest of the low."[114]

Why would God create a being so close to God and reduce him to such distance? The reason was love. God "loved to be known," and desired through man to have the greatest experience of knowing himself. This would only be possible if man was first removed from that awareness. If we are sitting in the Taj Mahal, we don't have the aspiration to go visit it. We only have such an aspiration if, to begin with, we are far away from it. Hence, by God distancing man from his God awareness, love for God was born, love in which man would strive to recognize himself and all of life in and as God.

This meant that man would seek and love God not just within himself, but also in all of life: in nature, in his neighbor,

---

[112] Claude Addas, "The experience and doctrine of love in Ibn 'Arabi," The Muhyiddin Ibn 'Arabi Society, trans. Cecilia Twinch, accessed August 18, 2015, http://www.ibnarabisociety.org/articles/addas1.html [emphasis mine].

[113] Qur'an 15:29 (Pickthall).

[114] Qur'an 95:4-5 (Pickthall).

in the poor, in the hungry, in the needy. All of life would become a source and destination of love for God. Krishna beautifully describes this as follows: "They alone see truly who see the Lord the same in every creature, who see the deathless in the hearts of all that die. Seeing the same Lord everywhere, they do not harm themselves or others. Thus they attain the supreme goal."[115]

One of the teachers who best exemplified this love in his teachings and his life was Jesus Christ. While summarizing the essence of all of God's teachings, Jesus gave two commandments to his disciples: "Thou shalt love the Lord thy God with all thy heart, and with all thy soul, and with all thy mind";[116] and "Thou shalt love thy neighbor as thyself."[117] Most intriguing is what's said by Jesus in between these two commandments: "This is the first and great commandment. And the second is like unto it."[118]

As per Jesus, the first commandment is "like" or "equal" to the second. Consequently, the three loves that are discussed in these two commandments are also equal:

Love for God = Love for the Neighbor = Love for Oneself

Since the word "neighbor" connotes all others in creation, the above equation changes to the following:

Love for God = Love for all others in creation = Love for Oneself

We defined love earlier as seeing the good, the spirit of God, in

---

[115] Easwaran, *Gita*, 13:27-28.

[116] Matthew 22:37 (KJV).

[117] Matthew 22:39 (KJV).

[118] Matthew 22: 38-39 (KJV).

another. Including this definition, we now have the following equation:

To see God as God = To see God in all others in creation = To see God in Oneself.

Therefore, as per these commandments, love for God equates to seeing God within oneself and within all of creation.

An equation by its nature is perfectly balanced. Therefore, love for God and seeing of his spirit also needs to be perfectly balanced between oneself and the rest of creation. Accordingly, in perfect unconditional love, the separation between God and his creation disappears. Wherever one turns, within or without, one sees the all-pervading presence of God,[119] and can only love and serve that God.

These commandments were exemplified in the life of Jesus. He had no enemies, he couldn't hate, even the ones who hated him. He saw the spirit of God in all. How could he hate his beloved? Jesus teaches us:

You have heard that it was said, 'Love your neighbor and hate your enemy.' But I tell you, love your enemies and pray for those who persecute you, that you may be children of your Father in heaven. He causes his sun to rise on the evil and the good, and sends rain on the righteous and the unrighteous. ... **Be perfect, therefore, as your heavenly Father is perfect.**[120]

If we exercise these commandments in our life, they have the potential to bring significant changes. Let us imagine that we go to our place of worship and raise our hands to say a prayer to God. As we leave to go home, we walk past despairing

---

[119] Qur'an 2:115 (Yusuf Ali).

[120] Matthew 5:43-48 (NIV) [emphasis mine].

members of the community and intentionally ignore them to avoid getting involved in their problems. This is a misalignment of love as per the above commandment because our love for God doesn't reflect on our love for others. Similarly, let us imagine doing great works and service for society. However, in performing this service, we ignore our own health, spirituality, our family, and others who depend on us. Again, this is a misalignment of love because our love for others doesn't reflect on our love for ourselves. We need to take care of the God without, as well as the God within. Love, hence, becomes the goal of all expressions of life, of aligning each self to its ultimate recognition as and in God.

In the Qur'an, God reminds humanity to strive for a heavenly afterlife by witnessing and believing in God and his teachings. Muhammad explains this belief in a very succinct way when he says: "You will not enter Paradise until you believe, and you will not (truly) believe until you love one another."[121] It's when we love one another, pay attention to the good in one another, see God in one another, that we truly enter paradise and live out the teachings of God. It's only then that we truly love God with all our heart, all our mind, and all our soul. There are no enemies in that love, just the spirit playing its many roles in the play of life with the objective to know itself. Eventually, the lover becomes the beloved, and the purpose of all life and living is fulfilled.

---

[121] "Sunan Ibn Majah-The Book of the Sunnah-Vol. 1, Book 1, Hadith 68," Sunnah.com, accessed August 18, 2015, http://www.sunnah.com/urn/1250680.

JOURNEY OF LOVE FOR GOD
STAGE 2: PREPARE

Focus your attention on a person or thing
you love in your life.
The feeling that arises is from God.

Voice of Man

Dear God, I'm unable to love you. My whole life, I have tried to love you, but I have been unsuccessful. You have always been a concept for me, never a reality. I have questioned you in the depths of my being. I have looked for you in every book and story about you. All I have seen, all I have witnessed is mankind trying to invent someone bigger than itself that explains all of life. It's true that even with all of our scientific advances, we can't explain most of life. We still don't understand fully the phenomena that we observe inside the atom or outside in space. Is there a God behind all of this? Perhaps, there is. But how can I love this God when even his identity is a "perhaps" for me?

Dear God, it wasn't always like this. I used to believe in you. I used to call you my invisible friend. My parents would see me talk to you all the time. During play time, I would even put out toys for you and say, "This is for God to play with." During lunch, I would make my mom put a plate for you on the table. When the food wouldn't disappear, I would tell my mom that you weren't hungry. Every time I would see a super hero, I would say, "He's good, but not as good as my God." When my parents got divorced, I cried many nights, telling you all the feelings I had in my heart. I felt that somehow I was responsible for their divorce, that I should have been a better child. Then maybe, just maybe, they would still be together. You were the center of my world, my secret, my support, my best friend.

Dear God, one day, I suddenly grew up. I realized that all those times that I had put out toys for you, you had not played; all those times I had put out food for you, you had not eaten. I realized that every time I called upon you, especially when in pain, you had not responded back. I was talking to an emptiness. I was talking to no one at all. You didn't really exist. You were a figment of my imagination that my parents and religious instructors had made me believe. Many children have imaginary friends when they are young to keep them company. Many children believe in Santa Clause to bring them gifts for Christmas. But this belief only lasts until the child is a child. I had finally grown up.

Dear God, even this dialogue seems silly to me. Who am I speaking with? God ... Really ... Is there anyone on the other side? Here I am, writing, speaking, and talking to a perception of you that exists in my mind. But are you really there? Ugh, I hate that feeling, that feeling that we are alone in the universe. It makes all of life worthless; it makes all of me exist for no reason. This is my last attempt to talk to you. If you can hear me God, please make yourself known.

Dear God, I now sit in silence seeking your guidance ... My heart stirs as I remember a story I had forgotten:

A neighbor once found Mullah Nasruddin on his hands and knees on the street searching for something. "What are you searching for Mullah?" asked the neighbor. "My key. I have lost it," Nasruddin replied. The neighbor joined the Mullah and they both kept searching. After a while the neighbor asked, "Where did you lose it?" Nasruddin replied, "At home." The neighbor was agitated, "For God's sake, why are you searching for it here then?" Nasurddin answered, "Because there's more light here."[122]

---

[122] Adapted from Anthony De Mello, "Searching In The Wrong Place," in *The Song of the Bird*, 2nd ed. (Anand, India: Gujarat Sahitya Prakash, 1982), 32.

Dear God, it was as if I was sinking in a pit of quicksand and this story gently pulled me out. I realized that I too had been looking for the key in the wrong place. It was not my belief in God that I had lost; it was my belief in love. When my parents got divorced, I stopped believing in love, for how could two people that loved each other hurt each other so much? When I stopped believing in love, I stopped believing in everything and everyone I loved. I stopped believing in you, the one I loved the most. Love is something we can't fully explain; it's something we can only experience. From childhood, I had experienced my parents' love for each other. But, when it turned into arguments and fights, when it turned into hate, I stopped believing that such a thing was real. I started believing that all these years, my parents had imagined that they loved each other. Respectively, I started believing that all these years, I had imagined that I loved you. Just like their love didn't exist anymore, my love didn't exist anymore. So, you didn't exist anymore.

Dear God, I realized that I didn't need to prove that you existed. I only needed to love again. I needed to love someone or something with all my heart, all my mind, and all my soul. As I did, I would find you again. As a child, I had this love for all of life, all the time, so I saw you everywhere. As an adult, when I lost this, I lost you, and I lost myself. I inherited those feelings of emptiness, loneliness, and separation from myself, from all of life.

Dear God, I decided to call my parents. I asked them to meet me at a coffee shop. As they sat in front of me, awkwardly looking at each other as if they were two strangers, I told them what was in my heart. "Mom and Dad, I only brought the two of you together to say one thing. Even if you don't love each other anymore, I still love the both of you. I want you to know that." As I said this, I got up and gave them both a tight embrace, one arm around each of them. Suddenly, love exploded in my heart. Tears flowed through my eyes as if a high pressure pipe had been unclogged. I felt myself dissolve as an inner softness overtook me. I felt my mom and dad also dissolve. They, too, had been holding on to pain, to separation, to a feeling of being empty and lost. In that moment, all of us found love. Finding love, we all found ourselves, we all found God.

JOURNEY OF LOVE FOR GOD
STAGE 3: ARRIVE

Imagine a time before your birth
when you existed as the spirit of God.
Connect with the feeling of infinite, unconditional love
you felt that moment for everyone and everything.

Voice of God

Mullah Nasruddin was once speaking of God to a crowd. One of the hecklers cried: "O Mullah, instead of spinning up spiritual theories, why don't you show us something practical?" Nasruddin humbly asked: "What kind of practical thing would you have me show you?" The heckler confidently spoke: "For example, show us an apple from the garden of paradise." Nasruddin immediately picked up an apple and handed it to the heckler. "But this apple is bad on one side. Surely, a heavenly apple would be perfect," the heckler noticed. "A celestial apple would, indeed, be perfect," the Mullah said, "but given your present faculties, this is as near to a heavenly apple you'll ever get."[123]

I am as you see me. This is why there's so much diversity in the way people see me. Every seer has his or her own perception of me. I am like water. I mold to whatever container you contain me in, you see me in. I am not contained by your definitions; your definitions are contained by me. This is why there are so many today that struggle to find me. They are trying to find me in the same way as their ancestors did. Your ancestors were using their own containers. You have to use your own. Every human being has been given his own eyes. Why do you strive to see me with the eyes of someone else

---

[123] Adapted from Anthony De Mello, "The Perfect Apple," in *The Song of the Bird*, 2nd ed. (Anand, India: Gujarat Sahitya Prakash, 1982), 202-203.

when you have been given sight yourself?

When you see me, you see yourself. I have created each of you unique, each of you my son or daughter in his or her own way. Even identical twins, though they may look alike, are very different from one another. Each of you is also unique. In your uniqueness, you express my uniqueness. In your diversity, you reflect my diversity. This is not just true for human beings. This is true for all of life. Each tree is different, unique. Each leaf is different, unique. Each bird, each bee, each ant, each grain of sand, even each raindrop has its own uniqueness, its own life, its own being. Life is meant to be a unique experience for every living being. When you try to deny your uniqueness, you try to deny me.

But, you have reached a time in history when life is built on categories. Whenever you encounter anything new, you strive first to name it and label it so that it belongs within all that you already know in life. You then give it a definition and an application so that you can agree or disagree on its understanding and utility in uniformity. I don't fit into this framework. Life, in which I am embodied, doesn't fit into this framework. Try not to analyze; instead, try to realize. See the mystic as he looks at a tree, a cloud, a ray of sunshine. See the child as he looks at a wave, a breeze, a drop of rain. See the mystery in their eyes as if they are seeing it each time for the first time. See the joy in their hearts as they live that moment that experience. I am inviting you back to this joy: to your personal unique experience of life, to your personal unique experience of me. I am inviting you back to your light, your infinite eternal light, your infinite eternal nature as love.

Ahh, love, how sweet it is! What is love? Love is that first burst of flavor you feel when you eat your favorite ice cream. Love is that first cool breeze of wind you feel on a hot and humid day. Love is that thrill and excitement in the pit of your stomach as the roller coaster climbs to the first drop. Love, my dear, is every moment of life that you are fully alive, that you are fully aware, that you are fully excited about and that you are fully embracing. Wherever love is, I am. Wherever I am, love is. Just as God is a name for all the diverse ways that man describes his source, love is a name for all the diverse experiences that man has of that source. This is why when you don't feel love, you don't feel me. When you don't experience love, you don't experience me. You forget your own essential nature. Life doesn't feel good to you. You feel far from life and life seems far from you.

In old times, I used to be a reality without a name. You loved me as beauty, you loved me as grace, you loved me as starlight, and you loved me as your beloved's face. I was the hunt in which you looked for food and prayed for the animal as he gave his life for your sustenance. I was the harvest in which you picked the grain and celebrated the rain with food and dance. I was present in every moment in every fraction of time. I lay in the sound of the thunder, in the cry of the wind.

But now, I am a name without a reality. You have labeled me and neatly organized me on a bookshelf. You have painted pictures of me and allowed me visitors at a museum. You have symbolized me and planted me deep in the places of worship. You have terrorized me and written my name on the shells of bullets. I am the giver of life, and you have labeled me the bringer of death. I am the joy of the heart, and you have labeled me grief and suffering. Let's stop. Let's begin again. Let's remember where this all started. Let's remember the time when you came into existence as eternal love, as eternal light.

I love you, my child, and I am waiting for you to find me in your life. You don't have to go on a long journey. Find love, and you'll find me. Find me, and you'll find yourself. As your love deepens, so will your experience of me, so will your experience of life, so will your experience of yourself. Then, every apple will be a heavenly apple, every moment a divine ONE.

JOURNEY OF LOVE FOR GOD
STAGE 4: EXPERIENCE

Experience feeling from the heart of God for all of life.
God has no enemies; all is a reflection of himself.

Voice of Muhammad Rasulullah
(Muhammad Messenger of God)[124]

I was getting ready to attend to my daily affairs. As I left my house, a very unusual site greeted me. The path that I took when leaving my house was clean. I expected it to be littered with trash, something that had been a daily occurrence. I said to myself: "Perhaps the neighbor woman has something else much worse planned for me today." I had suffered many abuses at the hands of the people of Mecca. They had thrown stones, animal entrails, blood, thorns, trash, sand, and branches at me. I had been pushed into holes, often filled with thorns and trash. Many times I had been physically hurt. But, it was not the physical ridicule and abuse that bothered me. It was that these were my people, my own family members, my uncles, my cousins, my near and dear, who were subjecting me to such hatred.

None of this stopped me from my mission. I had been given a message from my Lord, which was my duty to deliver and, above all, exemplify. It was a message of generosity and kindness, of love and mercy, especially for those who were the most marginalized of life: the poor, the orphan, the slave, and the hungry. It was a message of equality, giving honor and privilege to both man and woman so that both would be

---

[124] See Tanvir Kazmi, "The Garbage Thrower," ireport.cnn.com, accessed November 12, 2015, http://ireport.cnn.com/docs/DOC-1204985, and Aslan, *No God But God*, 39-49, to read more about the mistreatment of Muhammad by his community.

190

respected and celebrated at birth instead of one being preferred over the other. It was a message of peace and unity, of bringing all tribes and peoples under the protection and love of one God, of one reality, of one community. It was a message of responsibility, of each of us doing our part to make the lives of our fellow brothers and sisters better, especially if we had been given the means to do so. Of course, the Meccans didn't like this message. A thriving economy was built on all the vices that my message strived to correct. The Meccans didn't want to lose this economy, their status, their power, and their riches. Consequently, they did everything they could to deter me from my work.

As I continued to walk on the path under the house of my neighbor, I kept an eye towards the sky in case some debris would come raining down on me from her window. To my surprise, nothing of this sort occurred. This is when a thought struck me. Perhaps something was wrong with the woman. Immediately, my heart filled with concern for her. I closed my eyes and prayed: "Dear God, please attend to that woman as you attend to me and my family in every way." As I completed my prayer and opened my eyes, a servant girl walked out of the woman's house. I inquired about her mistress. She said that her mistress was very sick and unable to get out of bed. I inquired if her mistress was available to take visitors. She said yes and took me inside the house. As she announced me to her mistress, I clearly heard her mistress exclaim in a shaking voice: "What does he want? Has he come to pay me back for all those times I threw trash in his way? Tell him, I don't want to see him."

The servant girl returned with a dejected face. Before she could convey her mistress's message, I interrupted her. "Please tell your mistress, I am here as a friend. Please tell her that I wish to check up on her health and pray to God for her quick recovery." The woman was really sick and couldn't afford to turn away a friend or a prayer. I was invited into her room. Upon entering the room, I observed that she was burning up in fever. She was sweating from head to toe and even though covered in blankets, shivered like she was outside in the desert night. As she looked at me with her hazy eyes, she spoke to me in a soft tone. "After all I have done to you, Muhammad, will your God really save me?"

I felt the love of God embody my heart as it often did when another human being was in need, and I was supposed to help. My face broke into a smile that I only knew when the Lord worked through me in such ways. I asked the servant girl to give me a glass of water. I said a prayer, lifted the woman's head, and helped her drink the water. Holding her face in my hands, I looked at her, seeing her soul. To it, I spoke:

In the name of God, the Most Beneficent, the Most Merciful. I swear by the early hours of the day, And the night when it covers with darkness. Your Lord has not forsaken you, nor has He become displeased, And surely what comes after is better for you than that which has gone before. And soon will your Lord give you so that you shall be well pleased.[125]

As soon as I stopped speaking, the woman let out a great sigh. Her spirit was lifted, and she smiled back at me; she, too, had recognized the part of herself that I had seen in her. She held my hands and kissed them. Sleep overtook her and she fell back peacefully onto her bed.

As I walked out of the house, I silently said prayers upon prayers of gratitude. That day I knew that another soul had turned itself unto its Lord, had become a Muslim, submitting her will to God. Another soul had remembered the spiritual event when the Lord had said, "Am I not your Lord?" and all souls had answered, "Yes! we bear witness."[126] Certainly, my work had just begun. There would be many more days when

---

[125] Qur'an 93:1-5 (Shakir).

[126] Qur'an 7:172 (Shakir).

trash and abuse would be thrown at me and I would risk my life and my family's. But, I was beyond willing to go through that and more and be a messenger of God's love and mercy for all.

JOURNEY OF LOVE FOR GOD
STAGE 5: RELIVE

*O God, make me a channel of your love to all whom I
hold precious as well as I despise in my life.
All life begins and ends in your love.*

Voice of Shafeen

It was the evening of February 20, 2012. We were in one of
the post-delivery rooms at the Siratt Women's Center in
Bedford, Texas. My wife was finally getting some sleep after
thirty-six hours. The baby was sleeping next to her in the small
hospital carrier. I was a father. I didn't really know what to
feel. It had been an intense couple of days. My wife and I had
arrived at the hospital. My wife had endured hours and hours
of labor. There had been a few episodes where the baby had
trouble breathing and the staff had rushed in to change my
wife's position. As the child had finally arrived, the miracle of it
all stood larger than anything we had ever experienced before.
A parade of family members had paid visits. There were lots of
felicitations, lots of food, pictures, stories, and it was finally time
for mommy, baby, and daddy to sleep. But the baby had some
other plans.

Suddenly, waking up from the middle of her sleep, she
started crying. I lifted her out of her carrier and rocked her
gently but that didn't work. She wanted her mommy and
wanted to be fed. It was the first sleep that my wife had gotten
after going into labor. I wanted to let her sleep but had no idea
what to do with the crying baby. I looked around as if a nurse,
perhaps an angel, someone, anyone would rush in to help me.
But no help arrived. We didn't even have pacifiers. I felt
helpless. Suddenly, the Lord whispered in my heart, "Give the
baby your pinkie."

I put my pinkie in her mouth and she started sucking on it.

It was a beautiful moment. All through labor, my wife had done all the work to get this baby out. Even when it was out, the baby, having spent nine months in the mother's womb, desired her mother's warmth. She also wanted to be fed and only mommy could do that. I had felt left out wondering what role I served. Finally, I had found my role, the role of a dad, the role of a father. I said to the baby in my heart:

I'll always be there for you whenever you need me. I'll protect you from all harm. I'll watch over you every step of the way, always nearby just in case you need me. You'll always be loved, completely, unconditionally. You'll always know that you are loved: through all the hugs and kisses, through all the laughing and playing, through all the stories and running, through all the talks and listening. I'll always be there to listen to you, to hear what you have to say. You'll know that what you say is important, even if it's pointing something out, like a bird or a bug, for the twentieth time. When you fall, I'll be there to pick you up, to let you know that it will feel better soon. When you soar, I'll be there to encourage you, to let you know that it's your destiny to shine. I'll say to you: "Shine your eternal light so bright that it illuminates the entire world!"

Suddenly, I was struck with an intense feeling that my life in that moment was a mirror. My relationship with my daughter that instant was a reflection of the relationship of the Spiritual Father with me. The love I felt for my daughter that moment was a reflection of the love that the Spiritual Father felt for me. I had witnessed the Spiritual Father express his love in my life. He had nurtured me, strengthened me, protected me, listened to me, guided me, smiled with me, laughed with me, encouraged me, enlightened me, in summary LOVED me. Now, I was reflecting that love towards my daughter.

The relationship I have today with the Spiritual Father wasn't always there. There was a time in my youth when I only knew the Spiritual Father conceptually. He was a mystery, someone who was talked about, preached about, prayed to, and appreciated, but not really present. Almost twenty years ago in another hospital, all of that had changed. Amidst a great tragedy, I had experienced the presence and peace of the Spiritual Father.

It was May 17, 1993. We had received the news at 5:00 a.m. that my dad had passed away. We had raced to the Harbor-UCLA Medical Center in Torrance, California. As my older siblings and mom rushed inside to understand what had happened with my dad, I was left alone in the lobby. The hospital wouldn't let me enter the special care unit as I was a minor. I was wearing shorts that day. Even today, I can feel the coolness of the metal chair that I sat on in the lobby. Tears were streaming down my face. I was crying profusely. I had never truly understood my bond with my physical father until that day. He was a pillar in my life. Upon finding out that he was no more, the building of my life had come crashing down.

The grief in which I was absorbed in that moment was so deep that I had forgotten who I was. I only knew that I was sad and heartbroken. In the middle of my intense grief, something happened. Something opened up within my inner being. I had access to a presence that I had never felt before. It was complete peace, complete stillness, a presence beyond time and space. I was embraced by this peace as if I belonged there. Nothing existed outside of that peace. Even I didn't have a distinct existence. I was a part of the whole which it was.

This was that moment that my relationship with my Spiritual Father consciously began. I say consciously because he had always been there, watching me, directing the threads of my life, guiding me from within. It was just that I didn't know who or what that presence was until that moment in the hospital lobby. Before my dad died, I believe he had a conversation with my Spiritual Father. In that conversation, he requested that since he was leaving, his wife and kids be taken care of and be guided. He was particularly concerned about me, the youngest one, who had spiritual aspirations, and would need guidance in order to stay on the right path. Through his request, I believe my dad initiated my special relationship with the Spiritual Father and I was made to feel peace, a peace I would never forget.

Today, as many people ask for evidence to prove the existence of God, it feels strange to me. There's nothing truly one can ever do to satisfy one's mind-based need to prove God. Knowledge of his existence is hardwired in every individual soul; it's just that we are veiled from that knowledge. When the Spiritual Father graces us as such, we are able to see beyond that veil. That grace had touched my heart that moment. I would spend the rest of my life looking under that veil to find a deeper sense of the divine and of my own true self.

After thirty minutes of my daughter sucking my pinkie, I put her back in the hospital carrier. She cooed a little bit and went back to sleep. As I lied down to sleep as well, I reflected on how life was quickly changing for me. Here I was, entrusted with a spiritual child of the Spiritual Father, a child he trusted me to raise properly. I asked: "O Lord, you have already felt the love in my heart for this child. What else can I do to fulfill this trust that you have given to me?" I received the answer from the heart: "Dear son, do for this child as your dad did for you. Not as much through your words but rather through your example." I was reminded, then, of the many ways that my dad had guided me though his example.

As a child, I used to co-sleep with my parents. Whenever I would happen to wake up in the middle of the night around 4:00 a.m., I would see my dad sitting on a chair across the bed. He would be covered with a *chadar*, a bed sheet, like a mystic, seeking the Spiritual Father. When I was eight years old, I was keeping a fast as part of the Shia Ismaili Muslim faith called *Shukarwari Beej*. It had barely been half a day of fasting and I was starving. I approached my dad and said, "Dad, I'm hungry, what should I do?" Instead of telling me that it was a sin to break the fast or that he was disappointed in me or that God would be upset at me, my father simply pointed at a banana and said: "Eat." When we immigrated to the U.S., my dad would often take me to the park where we would play basketball together. He was forty years my senior and was on medicine for heart disease and yet he joined me. When we played basketball, he couldn't throw the ball over his shoulders so he would throw it underhand, and would always make that basket. He tried his best to learn every game I played, performing tasks beyond his physical and cultural comforts. He strived to be his son's best friend, even though we were two generations apart. After he died, whenever my dad's friends remembered him, they would always add: "Your father was a gold-hearted man. There aren't men like him anymore in life." I would aspire to be a good father, like my dad was, to me. I would aspire to be a good son, like my dad was, to the Spiritual Father.

As I fell asleep, I expressed gratitude for all the blessings that had unfolded in my life. "Thank you, Lord!" I whispered. The Lord replied: "You are most welcome, my son. Now, go to sleep, lots of work to do tomorrow." There would always be work to do and experiences to live. Not all of them would be filled with joy and happiness like the one I had just experienced. But the Spiritual Father would always be there to guide me and teach me to feel from his heart. That heart would be my compass as I fulfilled this journey of being a father, of being a son, of being God's love, of being God's light, in my life, in all life.

JOURNEY OF LOVE FOR GOD
STAGE 6: CONVERSE

My child, in my love, all is loved, all is complete.
The mirror reflects completely the one looking.

Voices of Man and God

Man: O God, what would you say to someone who says to you:

I'm in darkness, my Lord. I'm depressed, I'm worried, I'm stressed, and I'm suffering from a terminal illness. I have lost those who were most dear to me. I have been abused, I have been betrayed and cheated, and I have been hurt physically, mentally, emotionally, and spiritually. I have been starved, I have been caged, and I have been left alone to die. How can you expect me to love? How can you expect me to be lit? How can you expect me to shine? How can you expect me to have a hungry stomach and love others while they don't love me enough to feed me? How can you expect any of this from me, when even you, who brought me into this life, who sent me here as your light, have left me all alone, without support, without succor? How could you let me be surrounded by this darkness? How could you just watch while I was mistreated, while I was left alone? Why didn't you come to my help? Why weren't you there when everyone else left me?

God: My son, my daughter, my love! When you suffered, I suffered. When you cried, I cried. When you starved, I starved. When you fell, I fell. When it hurt you, I was hurting. When you felt alone, I felt alone. Every prick you felt, I felt. Everything and everyone you lost, I lost. You are the witness of life, while I am the one living this life. If the pain of the witness was so much, can you imagine my pain as the one actually living through it? God is not someone who watches over you from a distance while you go through life. God is not even someone who stays in the good while you suffer. God is the essence of life, the one to whom and through whom all life happens. So the hand that didn't feed you was mine but the stomach that was not fed was also mine. My suffering is beyond anyone's suffering, even yours. For you only feel your suffering, while I feel the suffering of all. Everyone who suffers, suffers in my heart, cries in my heart, and hurts in my heart.

And yet, I preach the message of love, of light. There's no other way out of darkness but light. You can mull over the darkness umpteen times but until and unless you focus on light, the darkness will remain. There's no other way to end your suffering and mine. There's no other way to find a hand that feeds you and feeds me. Believe in me, trust in me, I do this not just for you but also for myself. As you live your utmost, I am that utmost. As you become a being of light, I shine in your glory.

This light is your birth right. It was there before you came into physical existence. It will be there after you leave this physical existence. Remember this light as your essential nature, and let it shine, even in the direst of circumstances.

When this light shines from within, this light shines from without. It's as if what's within you is a homing beacon and as that beacon is lit, the light from which it emerged homes into it. Then you see the circumstances fade, the loneliness fade. Then you find a full stomach, not just from a material perspective but especially from a spiritual perspective. Your light lights the way for my light to shine, within as well as without. Those closest to my light are attracted by your light and come to your help. They show up in your life as my angels, as my blessings upon your life.

No one benefits from being in the darkness. You must be in the light to help yourself, to help others. And no one, not even me, can bring you into this light, until and unless you choose this light for yourself. Of course, a hundred forms of encouragement can be made available to you: good people preaching and showing the example of the good to you. But until and unless you choose goodness, love, and light, for yourself, your life will not change. An addict can be entered into hundreds of addiction removal programs and still go back to his addiction. Until and unless he lights the light of freedom from all substances within himself, he's not able to fully utilize the light, the good within him and around him. Darkness is an addiction as well. Negativity and despair is an addiction as well. No matter how much light surrounds it, unless lit from within, this darkness and despair continue.

Man: O God, how can one love you and also love themselves? How can one love you, love themselves, and also love their family? How can one love you, themselves, their family, and still love society? How can one love you, themselves, their family, their society, and yet love their jobs, their careers, their businesses? I feel there's so much conflict in this way of love. Ultimately, love is an expression that seems to me bounded by time and time is limited more and more in the society we live in today. If we are so strapped for time, how can we truly love and spend time on and with others?

God: When you love me unconditionally, you love yourself. When you love yourself, you love your family. When you love your family, you love your society. When you love your society, you love every aspect of life in that society including running your business or attending to your job. You even love attending a Christmas or Hanukkah or Eid or Diwali celebration and being with your fellow spiritual brothers and sisters. All love comes back to me. All love originates in me. This is not a matter of time and the amount of time spent on an activity or a person. That's a utilitarian way of looking at life. That's only one way of measuring life, a way that though logical lacks the perception to truly see my grandness and form. I am present in the essence of life and the essence of life is not time bound. The essence of life is immeasurable, infinite, and eternal.

It's like you go to a grocery store and you give $5. The

grocery owner gives you a bag of rice, a bag of potatoes, a bag of tomatoes, a bag of strawberries, a bag of lentils, a bag of onions, a bag of apples, a bag of carrots, a bag of meats, and a bag of peppers. You look back and say, all of that is $5. He says yes, each is $5 and because you gave me $5, I must give you all of them. But I only paid for one, you say. But this is not any ordinary grocery store. You paid for one, but you earned all ten. Such is my love. When you love me, you earn love in all of those categories that you summarized earlier. When you love any of those categories with my love, you love all of them while loving only one of them.

Again, this won't make sense to you if you try to measure this from a logical perspective. God's love can't fit within the reason of mankind. Jesus gave the example of workers in a field who would be paid the same amount for the entire day regardless of whether they started since morning or joined in the afternoon or joined in the evening.[127] That makes no logical sense. It makes complete sense from the point of view of love.

My only desire is to be loved by you. When you fulfill this one desire for me, I fulfill all desires of love for you. Life loves you when you love me. Everywhere you go, the flowers, the trees, the birds, look forward to your arrival. They sing for your presence because they feel in your heart your love for me and your love for all of life. I am all of life. When you love me, you love life, and life loves you back.

It won't matter then that you only spend an hour a week with your parents. That hour will be filled with my spiritual abundance and will mean more to your parents than an entire week of you being with them. In this way, time becomes negligible as infinity helps every moment carry eternal power for you. That power comes from love. It comes from the love you have for me and the love I have for you. Ultimately, all love for God is self-love for what are you if not me. I desire your love because I desire you knowing yourself as me. The quickest and

---

[127] Matthew 20:1-16 (NIV).

the best way for you to know yourself as me is to love me. As the lover disappears into the beloved, there is nothing left but me.

Man: O God, there are people in our lives who we love more than others: our spouses, our children, our parents. Sometimes we even love them more than you, at least from a worldly perspective. We sometimes only pray to you because we desire the good of those we love. So, even our love for you seems conditional on the love we have for those family members or others. Is this wrong for us to do? Is there a better way for us to love?

God: Not at all, my child. Any form of sincere, deep love is good love. But I do want to separate love from attachment. Love is good and so it makes you feel good. When you hurt because a loved one doesn't love you back, what you feel in that moment is not love. I want to clarify this because many people have justified killing themselves or others in the name of love. This is not the way that I have taught. Love is completely free, free within, and free without. Love is completely unconditional, it doesn't require any recompense, and it doesn't require any response. Love is completely free of judgment, it doesn't love only and unless one acts or speaks a certain way.

I can hear you saying that this means that most people don't truly love others because almost all people are filled with judgment for others. This is true. But this doesn't mean that there aren't glimpses of unconditional love within the conditioned love. Each couple, each parent and child, each group of friends, has those beautiful unconditional moments in their relationship. In fact sometimes years of relationships between two people or groups of people are sustained by such a moment or experience. They so value that moment or experience between each other that they "put up with" the rest of the judgment or nagging or whatever you want to call it.

Such is the power of unconditional love that one human has for another. Can you imagine if instead of being a moment, instead of an individual spending thirty seconds of their day in a state of unconditional love, they spent hours? What kind of transformation would they bring into their own life and the lives of others? Such a love is divine love. Such a love can only exist and originate from me. And when you love from that place, when you pray for others from that place, you have to have first gone through me. In that love, you are always with me. It's always right.

Even if it's conditioned love, it's an attempt, a preparation for divine love and so I love that love because my love, is unconditional. It can't be wrong in my eyes. For it to be wrong, I have to judge it and for me to judge your way of loving would make me conditional in my love towards you.

I love you just the way you are. This doesn't mean that I don't have aspirations for you to come closer to your goodness, to your light, to the unconditional love within you. But having aspirations is not the same as having conditions. When a parent desires good for his child, he/she loves the child regardless of whether that child achieves that good. It's the parent's role as a parent to desire and see the child always in the good. Even if the child struggles to demonstrate, the parent still loves him/her. That's what I mean when I say that I have aspirations for you but my aspirations aren't conditions on my love. On the contrary, my aspirations are more proof of the love that I have for you and for all my spiritual children. I desire for each of you what I desire for myself: to be one with my presence, with my complete being-ness. Becoming one, I desire for you to live a full, complete, love filled and light filled, life.

JOURNEY OF LOVE FOR GOD
STAGE 7: REALIZE

I now fly the kite of my life
with clear love for God.
I go wherever his love takes me
and his love grows wherever I go.

Voice of Reader

As I return back to my day to day life, I reflect on the following questions to apply lessons from this journey:
- What new insights did I receive through this journey about life and about God?

- What changes will I make in my daily life as a result of these new insights?

- How will these changes help me live a more fulfilled and meaningful life?

Journey of Union with God

God as the Goal of devotee

Life in the ultimate analysis has taught me one
enduring lesson. The subject should always
disappear in the object. ... And in the highest
realms of consciousness all who believe in a
Higher Being are liberated from all the clogging
and hampering bonds of the subjective self in
prayer, in rapt meditation upon and in the face of
the glorious radiance of eternity, in which all
temporal and earthly consciousness is swallowed
up and itself becomes the eternal.

— Sir Sultan Muhammad Shah,
Memoirs of Aga Khan

JOURNEY OF UNION WITH GOD
STAGE 1: ASPIRE

Remember God all the time to
re-member yourself with God.
Then peace emanates through you
and all of life partakes in it.

Voice of Shafeen

A mystic had meditated for years and years in his search for the ultimate goal. Finally, one night, he arrived at the home of God. He knocked. A voice asked, "Who's there?" The mystic replied, "It's I, your servant. Please, open the door, and let me in." The voice responded, "There's only room for one in here." The imagery disappeared, and the mystic found himself awake in his humble hut. He was devastated. After years, when the fruit of his search was so near, God had denied him entry. He sought out his teacher, his spiritual guide. The teacher handed the mystic a small piece of folded paper. The mystic unfolded the paper and read what was written. It perplexed him much. However, when his eyes met those of his teacher's, what was written was immediately felt and understood. Again, the mystic began his practice. He meditated, and one night, again, he arrived at the home of God. He knocked. A voice asked, "Who's there?" The mystic replied, "It's you!" The door was opened. As the mystic entered, a small piece of paper was let go from his hands and landed on the door sill as a welcome sign for all those who were to enter. On it were written four words: "Die Before You Die."[128]

Today, more and more of us are fascinated by death. We see death as an event when the veils are lifted and we finally realize

---

[128] Adapted from Anthony De Mello, S. J., "Who Am I?," in *The Song of the Bird*, 2nd ed. (Anand, India: Gujarat Sahitya Prakash, 1982), 126-127.

the truth of life. Is there a God? Is there an afterlife? What happens to people once they die? There are many websites and books today that deal with death, as well as near death experiences. But often, in our fascination with it, we miss the point of death. It's a reminder for life. It reminds us to turn towards our life and ask the big questions: "Where did I come from?" "Why am I here?" "Where am I headed?" The mystic in the story above knows the answer. He knows that he has come from God and to God is his return.[129] While he's here on earth, he sees his purpose as union with God. He has, therefore, devoted himself to a search and remembrance of his true self, of the essence of all of life. He's striving to die to his temporary self and wake up to his eternal self before he physically dies.

In this journey of "Union with God," we strive to unite with our source, our creator, with the spirit of God, within and without. The act of achieving this union has been referred to differently by the teachers of God. The Buddha referred to this as "Nirvana." Muhammad called this "Companionship on the High." Rama and Krishna called this the "Supreme Goal" or the "Supreme Self." Socrates referred to it as the "company of gods." Jesus called this the "Kingdom of God." Moses' entire life journey was a physical representation of this spiritual "promised land." No matter what it's called, it's the ultimate goal of each believer of God in his/her eternal life. Accordingly, the best definition of God in this journey is GOD as the Goal Of Devotee.

The etymology of the word "goal" implies a "limit" or a "boundary." In this journey, the goal is the door, the boundary or the limit, beyond which nothing exists besides God. All seekers like the mystic above are devoted to crossing this boundary, to die before they die. There's a covenant made between each soul and its source that it would venture out into creation to experience it, and having fulfilled that experience,

---

[129] Qur'an 2:156 (Pickthall).

return back to its source. There's no other purpose to life except this. The teachings of God describe the process we must undertake to fulfill this covenant, to achieve union with God. Moreover, the life of the soul doesn't end after this union. On the contrary, it truly begins anew, as the one who returns becomes the means, a gateway, for others to return and find union.

There's a very mysterious statement in the Qur'an that serves as an inspiration to many mystical traditions. God says, "Remember Me, I will remember you."[130] The best way to demystify this verse is to break up the word remember into "re" and "member." Consequently, the word means to "put back together" or "reunite." As man re-members or re-unites himself with God, God re-members or re-unites man with himself. In a tradition attributed to God, delivered through Muhammad, God says:

I am as My servant thinks I am. I am with him when he makes mention of Me. If he makes mention of Me to himself, I make mention of him to Myself .... And if he draws near to Me an arm's length, I draw near to him a cubit, and if he draws near to Me a cubit, I draw near to him a fathom. And if he comes to Me walking, I go to him at speed.[131]

The experience that follows is one where man enters the place of God-consciousness, and God enters the place of man-consciousness as both of them merge into a unified experience of life.

Remembrance of God is a common practice requested of believers in the diverse teachings of God. For example, the

---

[130] Qur'an 2:152 (Pickthall).

[131] "40 Hadith Qudsi – Hadith 15," Sunnah.com, accessed November 12, 2015, http://sunnah.com/qudsi40.

Qur'an also says: "So remember the name of thy Lord and devote thyself with a complete devotion."[132] The Old Testament says: "You shall remember the Lord your God"[133]; and "I remember your name in the night, O Lord, and keep your law."[134] Krishna, speaking from God-consciousness, says in the Bhagavad Gita: "I am easily attained by the person who always remembers me and is attached to nothing else."[135]

This process of remembering is different from traditional notions of prayer or worship where man asks God for something. This remembering, instead, is meditating on our essential reality. It may involve the following:

- focusing on a word or a group of words
- focusing on the breath
- focusing on the physical body, senses, thoughts or feelings
- focusing on a form, an image, or a sound, within or without

In each case, the object of the focus usually feels natural to the individual and is aligned with his/her understanding or experience of God. The essence of all focusing is seeking the supreme reality, leaving behind all sense perceptions, and penetrating into that deeper reality.

Krishna succinctly describes this process in the Bhagavad-Gita: "Seek the Self in inner solitude through meditation. With body and mind controlled ... constantly practice one-pointedness, free from expectations and attachment to material possessions."[136] Through this process, the Higher Self within is

---

[132] Qur'an 73:8 (Pickthall).

[133] Deuteronomy 8:18 (ESV).

[134] Psalm 119:55(ESV).

[135] Easwaran, *Gita*, 8:14.

[136] Ibid., 6:10.

found. Krishna further explains: "In the still mind, in the depths of meditation, the Self reveals itself. Beholding the Self by means of the Self, an aspirant knows the joy and peace of complete fulfillment."[137]

Through this remembrance, the ultimate ignorance of one's true reality is healed. The Buddha teaches his followers: "O monks, I do not see any other single obstacle, hindered by which humanity for a long, long time fares up to heaven and down to hell and wanders on from world to world, like this obstacle of ignorance."[138] As we remember God and are re-membered by God, the duality ceases to be, and the two become one. God comes to live in us, and we come to live in God. That state of being occurs, which Jesus describes as, "I am in the Father and the Father is in me."[139]

The journey doesn't end there. Once integrated into God's essence, we become emissaries of his peace, love, and joy. Muslim mystics call this state Baqaa-billah, which means in Arabic, "eternal life in God." A stillness and serenity surrounds us. We join the ranks of those who are called gurus, masters, and teachers pointing the way to oneness and unity with the ultimate reality. In our unity with the supreme self, we become gateways to God, embodying and representing God's love, light, and mercy to all. God indicates Muhammad, as one such being in the Qur'an, when he says: "And We have not sent you [O Muhammad] but as a mercy to the worlds."[140]

Once, the great teacher Hanuman was gifted with a necklace of rare pearls by Sita, the queen who Hanuman referred to as Mother. Sita's husband, Rama, was a gateway to God for Hanuman. Hanuman considered Rama his Lord and meditated

---

[137] Easwaran, *Gita*, 6:20.

[138] Mitchell, *Buddha*, 75.

[139] John 14:11 (NIV).

[140] Qur'an 21:107 (Shakir).

upon Rama's name to re-member himself with God. Upon receiving the necklace, Hanuman cracked open pearl after precious pearl, looking for his Lord, Rama, within them. When asked to explain his strange behavior, Hanuman said:

> This is a gift from Mother, so it must have some value. I'm just testing to see what that may be. True, such beads glitter, and people sell them for a lot of money. But does that indicate real worth? According to what I've learned, something has true value if it contains, within it, the Lord. So I'm just searching to see whether or not these stones contain him. But I don't find him, therefore their glitter seems like darkness to me.[141]

One of the courtiers jested whether Hanuman's body was of value, whether it contained his Lord. Regarding this as a valid question, Hanuman clawed at his chest and ripped it apart exposing his beating heart. Inside his heart, the entire assembly saw Rama and Sita enthroned. Also, on every cell of Hanuman's body, they saw the presence of the name of his Lord: "Rama."[142]

This is the re-membrance we strive for as we strive for union with God. In such a remembrance, we die to ourselves, and we live only in God. The glitters of the world, the physical delights and richness, don't hold any worth for us unless they espouse the Lord within. We live our life to only see and experience the Lord. As we die to the temporal self, the Lord re-members himself with Himself, the individual self with the Supreme Self, the drop with the ocean. All is united and all is integrated, into one, a one without any other.

---

[141] Philip Lutgendorf, *Hanuman's Tale: The Messages of a Divine Monkey* (New York, NY: Oxford University Press, 2007), 156.

[142] Ibid.

JOURNEY OF UNION WITH GOD
STAGE 2: PREPARE

Find a word which reminds you of God
and remember it all the time.
The effect of that word in your heart and thoughts
brings you closer and closer to God.

Voice of Man

Dear God, it has been seven days since I last prayed. I just don't feel like praying anymore. It's not that I'm rebelling against you or that I don't believe in you, it's just that I don't understand anymore why I'm praying. For forty-five years, I have been a believer in you. My father used to take me to the place of worship when I was very little, and every day I did as he showed me. As I grew up, I was told that I needed to learn the word of God, so I read it from beginning to end and memorized most of it. I was told that there were certain things you liked and other things you didn't. My entire life, I have only done what you like and have abstained from every single thing that you dislike. I have never lied, never cheated, and never even looked at a woman with wrong intent. From the clothes I wear, to my beard, from the way I greet and express joy, to the food that I eat, from the woman who I married, to the kids that I had with her—everything has been done either in your name, inspired by your word, or done as per your liking.

Dear God, I'm tired of obeying you. I live in a world in which aggression and cruelty is rewarded and simplicity and peace looked down upon. I live in a world where the wrong is not just done in a closed room but is advertised on big billboards everywhere. I live in a world in which lying and cheating is everywhere, and one can't get ahead unless one plays by those rules. Your obedience has made me an outsider in this world. Why did you make me a faithful man in a world without faith? Why did you make me your follower in a world without your leadership?

Dear God, either take me away from this life or let me end my life. I'm so tired of this life. It's one thing when outsiders mock oneself, yet another when one's own family does it. Though I have worked night and day my entire life, my wife continues to compare me with others' husbands. She often says: "Why can't you be like him? Look at the car he drives, the home his family lives in, the schools his kids attend, the clothes and jewelry his wife wears?" My kids continue to compare me with their friends' dads. They often ask me: "But my friend's dad bought her a new car when she turned sixteen. Why can't you?" I have lived a simple life as per your word and have preached the same to my family. But because of this, I have become an outsider to those whom I call my own. I can't take it anymore. I can't pray to you anymore. For what purpose is my prayer, is my faith, if it can't even give me a dignified life?

Dear God, I now sit in silence seeking your guidance ... My heart stirs as I remember a story I had forgotten:

A mystic was meditating by a river bank when a man interrupted him. "Master, I wish to become your disciple," the man said. "Why?" asked the Master. "Because I want to find God," the man replied. The Master grabbed the man's had and pushed it under water. The man struggled desperately to break loose. After some time, the Master finally let go. The man fell on the river bank gasping for air while coughing up water. When the man had recovered, the Master asked: "What did you want most of all when you were under water?" The man replied, "Air!" The Master advised: "Come back to me when you want God the way you wanted air."[143]

---

[143] Adapted from John Suler, "Wanting God," Zen Stories to Tell Your Neighbors, accessed November 12, 2015, http://truecenterpublishing.com/zenstory/wantgod.html.

Dear God, it was as if I was drowning and this story gave me a new breath of life. Like the man, I, too, had pursued God all my life. But, my pursuit had been shallow founded on prescribed actions and deeds rather than original thoughts and feelings. This shallow faith had been extinguished not having any real reason over forty-five years for its own existence. I finally understood what it means to have true faith. I finally realized what it means to pursue God. True faith is not just completing a bunch of prescribed actions; it's gasping every moment for God, looking for him both in the world, as well as in one's heart and soul. It's the re-memberance of oneself with God. So much so, that everything else and everyone else seems illusory, a background, which only exists until one finds God and loses himself in him.

Dear God, now, I continue to pray but it's different. I have a reason to pray. Prayer is the means through which I commune with my beloved. It's no longer about how many prayers I offer but rather how I feel each time I offer my prayers. I also realize now that I need more time alone, away from the world to develop my relationship with you. I find this time in the early mornings when no one disturbs me. Instead of saying prayers during that time, I just take a word that represents for me the essence of everything that you are. I repeat this word silently in my heart, over and over again, from fifteen minutes to an hour. I find this ritual to be the most satisfying, out of everything else I do, to live out my relationship with you.

Dear God, I now seek and find you every day. Every moment I find empty, I fill it with the word, which for me represents your essence. My life has become full with your presence and has never been better. My happiness, joy, and peace penetrate everyone I live my life with, at home, at work, at my place of worship. I finally live a dignified life, a life worth living, living for you, living in you, living through you!

JOURNEY OF UNION WITH GOD
STAGE 3: ARRIVE

Offer peace to all with whom you engage in life.
That peace is inspired from remembrance of God and
remembrance of God is sustained by that peace.

Voice of God

There were four moths that were attracted to a flame. The first moth saw a world beyond the flame. It ignored the flame and went on its way to explore that world. The second moth saw the light of the flame and was satisfied with the knowledge of the flame's existence. It also went on its way. The third moth saw the light of the flame but desired to know it further, so it flew closer. It felt the heat of the flame and was satisfied with the experience of the flame's nature. It also went on its way. The fourth moth saw the light of the flame, flew closer and experienced the heat of the flame, but yet yearned to know and experience it even further. It flew closer and closer and closer until it entered the flame. It burned in the middle of the flame and was extinguished into the truth of the flame's essence. There were then three moths left that were attracted to the flame. All who seek me are like these four moths with I being the eternal flame.

Some seekers are like the first moth. They believe the physical life to be the ultimate reality. Accordingly, they believe that their home, job, family, status, and wealth are the ultimate objective for which to live. Often, these seekers try to prove my existence through a physical framework. After a lot of trial and error, they discover that there's no way to objectively prove that God exists. Consequently, they assume that only material life is real and worth believing and acting upon.

Some seekers are like the second moth. These seekers do believe in me intuitively and seek out my light. They find this light and presence of God in nature if not in scripture. Through their recognition, they live a life guided by my light but seek not to understand the nature of this light. They are content with knowing that they are well guided and have access to a framework (religious, social, cultural, philosophical, or personal) under which to live out their life on earth.

Some of the seekers are like the third moth. These believers crave an experience of my essence. They seek to know me beyond scripture, beyond ritual, beyond appearance, and beyond perception. They seek to feel me pulsating in their being. These are the ones who follow spiritual and mystical paths to acquire closeness to me. They reflect on the esoteric meaning of scripture, partake in personal development programs, strive for goodness and Godliness within themselves, and practice different forms of yoga (from *yuj*, in Sanskrit, which means "to bind" or "to unite") to engage the body, mind, and soul. In due time, they experience a vision or a feeling of my essence. Once they receive this experience, they are content with touching once the holy grail of all life. They live out the rest of their life either celebrating that moment or teaching others to acquire the same for themselves.

Some of the seekers are like the fourth moth. These are the ones that long for extinction in me. For these seekers, there's no other purpose to life or living. As long as they are separated from the eternal flame, they are like wild birds encaged in a city home. These moths know that their existence as a moth itself is a barrier to their knowing and experience of the flame. They know that the only way to acquire the flame is to give up and burn every aspect of their separate identity into the flame. This burning gives them true peace in their soul. When someone dies, people often say, "May the deceased rest in peace." This is the peace these seekers strive for while they are physically alive. They are mere shells, bodies whose minds and souls are sustained by me, and are at rest in my peace. To the external eye, they may appear as any other man or woman pushing a grocery cart, or a stroller, or giving a hug to their child when dropping them at school. But, in their heart, my great eternal flame burns, turning all their doing, seeing, and being into my doing, seeing, and being.

Every human being has been intended to be the fourth moth, to eventually burn in my eternal essence, and to rest in my eternal peace. As you live the eternal life of the soul, you eventually make your way from being the first moth, to the second, to the third, to the fourth, and finally to eternal peace. Because it's a journey that's unique to each human being, each takes his/her own way and own time to achieve it. I have eternity, so I wait, lit with the flame of love, waiting for each of you to return home. When you were separated from my being, you were encoded with directions and aspirations to return home. However, as each ventured into life, each found himself/herself at a different level of remembrance of those directions and aspirations.

As you go deeper in your remembrance of me, the original encoded instructions surface. Thereafter, you find a deeper knowing and experience of the flame within and without. As you enter that flame, eternal peace envelops you as you finally return to your essential home. Then, as you return to daily life, you become that peace—a gateway to God—for every other moth that crosses your path, hence, my path.

I love you, my child, and I wait every second, every moment, to re-member you to me and me to you. Entering the flame is a process of peeling all the layers that separate you from the flame, from my essence. Be patient in this process of giving yourself to me. If you don't experience peace and oneness right away, don't give up. Even the desire for oneness is an obstacle to oneness itself, for it reminds you of your separation from me and creates more distance. Continue to re-member me without any attachment to the outcome. You'll see my light penetrate your life, slowly at first, then deeper and deeper, until all you'll see will be my light, and all you'll be will be my light.

JOURNEY OF UNION WITH GOD
STAGE 4: EXPERIENCE

*Experience a divine wedding in which
you give yourself to God.
Merging into his essence, you truly
rest in peace and become peace.*

Voice of Shri Hanuman[144]

I was at the feet of my Lord. Now that he was back in the palace, there were so many to serve him, and my ability to come to his service was far reduced. Yet, I loved sitting at his feet, watching his effulgent face bestowing light and blessings all the time. I doubted that anyone saw what I saw of the Lord. If they did, they would join me at his feet and never leave him for a moment. It was night now, and I followed my Lord and Mother Sita to their bed chamber. As was the usual custom, I would have to leave them at the entrance. I had never understood why Mother Sita was allowed at night to retire into the bed chamber with my Lord, while I was forbidden. That night I finally got the courage to ask. I asked: "Dear Lord, why is it that I can't enter your bed chamber while Mother Sita can?"

My Lord smiled innocently and pointed at the line of Sindur, the red vermillion paste, that mother was wearing in the center of her head. Next, he and Mother Sita entered the room, and the door was closed behind them. The whole night, as was my custom, I sat on the roof of the palace, remembering the Lord with his name, "Rama, Rama, Rama." But, tonight, no matter how much I concentrated, one thought kept me distracted. What was so special about this Sindur?

The next morning, the first opportunity I got, I went to see

---

[144] See Lutgendorf, *Hanuman's Tale*, 157, to read more about the story of Hanuman "Covered with Sindur."

Mother Sita. I often visited her when I was hungry, and she fed me like my own mother would until I was full. As I stepped into her dressing room, I happened to catch her adorning herself with the Sindur. "Hanuman, I am almost done. Give me a few moments, and I'll have your meal setup for you," Mother graciously said. "Mother, I have a question for you. What's the meaning of the Sindur that you wear on your head?" I asked.

Mother smiled innocently just like my Lord had. She answered, explaining to me clearly: "The Sindur signifies the bond of wedlock between your Lord and me. Through this bond, we have become one with each other, not just physically, but also in our heart and soul. As I wear this Sindur every day, I reaffirm that relationship and pray for the longevity of his life and our relationship."

The words, "we have become one with each other," echoed in my being. I could think of nothing else. Though mother offered me food, I was not able to eat. All I could feel was this new found pain of being separated from my Lord. How could I be wed with my Lord? How could I become one with him in my heart and soul like my mother? Every moment, every breath, every atom in my being, affirmed: "Rama, Rama, Rama, Rama, Rama, Rama, Rama." Yet, here I was farther from the Lord than my mother because she was wed to him, and I was not. I started saying the Lord's name as I often did when faced with any difficulty. I asked him in my heart the solution to this problem. The Lord answered, and a smile broke out on my face. I rushed to the first Sindur shop I could find in the marketplace. I tore open many sacks of Sindur and dumped them all over my body. I lied down on the ground and rolled around in the Sindur until I was red from head to toe and to the tip of my tail. Quickly I rushed back to the court and took my spot at the feet of the Lord.

The Lord was reading something and didn't notice my state. All the courtiers did and started gasping and laughing. Mother Sita couldn't believe her eyes either and smiled innocently at me.

Finally, my Lord noticed the uproar in the court and glanced at me. He asked: "Hanuman, what happened to you? Why are you red from head to toe and to the tip of your tail?"

I joined the palms of my hand, and as my eyes welled up with tears, I spoke my heart's request: "Dear Lord, in every way, you are one with me except for the Sindur that adorns the head of Mother Sita. Therefore, I have covered every inch of my being with the same Sindur. Please accept me fully in your being as I accept you in mine."

That moment, tears welled up in my Lord's eyes also. He stepped off from the throne and embraced me with his heart. He whispered in my ears: "O Hanuman, you are never separate from my being in any way or form. The world has many rituals and forms for oneness, but the Lord only knows and sees the heart. Your heart is fully immersed in mine as mine is fully immersed in yours. You have no need to do anything else to be one with your Lord."

I took again my place at the feet of my Lord. I kept my eyes fixed on him as my heart remained fixed on his name, "Rama, Rama, Rama, Rama, Rama, Rama, Rama." I had been hailed and praised in the entire kingdom for my knowledge, strength, courage, devotion, and might. But, only I truly knew the secret of all of my doings. It was my Lord: his knowledge, his strength, his courage, his devotion, and his might. All I did, all I had done, was to take his name all the time. Though I didn't sleep much, even when I did, my soul said his name over and over again. My Lord had transformed my entire being such that what I said were his words, what I did were his deeds, what I possessed was his might and his power. Hanuman was nothing more than a mere vessel for the Lord's will.

As I thought these thoughts, the Lord looked at me and smiled. He could see everything in my being and knew exactly what I was thinking in that moment. I, too, smiled hearing his thoughts that moment. He was saying back to me: "Wherever you are, Hanuman, I will always be. As I will never be estranged from you, you, too, will never be estranged from me!"

JOURNEY OF UNION WITH GOD
STAGE 5: RELIVE

O God, unite me with the peace of your being.
My life is for you and you alone.

Voice of Shafeen

It was the evening of July 10, 2006. I was serving as the Uniformed Volunteers Team Lead at my place of worship in Torrance, California. It was my role to lock the door once all the attendees as well as the custodians of the place of worship had left. That day, I had to be somewhere so I asked one of the custodians if it was okay for me to leave early and someone else to close up. He told me: "No, we need to talk to you first about something. Can you please go to the second room in the lobby? We will meet you there."

His comment struck great worry in my heart. The next day was July 11. That was the day when volunteers for different responsibilities at the place of worship were appointed every year. The process involved the submission of names by previous position holders, selections by either the local council for our religious community or our spiritual leader himself, depending on the position, with the appointments being made public on July 11. The selected volunteers were usually told the day before about their appointments. This is why I was so worried. I was aware that my name had been submitted for a position serving as one of the custodians of the daily morning worship at our center between 4:00 a.m. and 6:00 a.m. The term would be from July 2006 through July 2007. Of all the positions, this was one of the most challenging, as it required an ultimate lifestyle discipline of waking up that early and attending to prayers.

In most circumstances, this would be great news. However, the upcoming year was already set to be a challenging one. Between work, school, family, and other volunteer services, to which I was committed, my plate was already full. I had no room to take on an additional responsibility, especially one like this which seemed so overwhelming. As I walked into the room where I was to wait, I noticed a poster on one of the walls. That room was a multi-purpose room which was used for religious education during the weekend and administrative activities during the week. A child had drawn and taped a poster to the wall with two words clearly highlighted. The words were "ISLAM NOW."

These words penetrated to the depths of my being. The Lord was speaking to me through that poster. He was telling me something that I had only come to understand recently: ISLAM, meaning "submit to the will of God," NOW meaning "right now, in this situation, in this problem, in this moment." If there's a philosophy that I can specify that describes the journey of finding meaning and purpose in my life, it would be these two words. That moment, I realized that I had to give my life to the Lord right then and there. Through many teachings and guidance in my life, I had already come to believe that I belonged to my Lord. However belief is one thing, action is another. Now was the time to truly act in accordance with what I believed.

All of our life, we are raised in a society that teaches us to think with our heads. It teaches us to be competent, to hold ourselves accountable, and to manage our time well. It tells us that we should only take on projects which we truly feel we can fulfill, to think before we act. That moment the Lord was telling me something that was counter to everything I had learned. He was saying: "I need you to act before you think. I need you to take a leap of faith before you see anyone or anything that will hold you or protect you. I need you to have complete trust in me and submit to my will for you, this moment, right now!"

As a child, I remember doing something similar when I had to learn how to ride a bike. A friend of mine had gotten a new bike and had learned to ride it. He offered it to us so that we, too, could do the same. The bike didn't have any training wheels and none of us knew how to ride it but we were told it was simple. Our friend said: "Just get on it and start peddling and turn when you reach a corner or something comes in your way." The instructions were too simple to capture the complexity required to balance and navigate a bike. Yet, they worked. Each of us fell off many times. We ran straight into walls because we couldn't remember to turn and balance at the same time. After many bruises, many falls, somehow it worked. We learned to ride the bike just by putting our faith in our friend who told us that it would be simple. As an adult, that kind of simplicity is considered stupidity. Why fall when you can avoid it? Why risk getting hurt when you can make sure that you won't?

That moment in the room, the Lord was asking me to be a child again. The Lord was asking me to trust in him, the friend who had ridden the bike and knew that I would be able to learn it. Inspired by "ISLAM NOW," I said in my heart, "*Aameen Khudavind*," which literally means "so shall it be, my Lord." That instant, the custodians of the place of worship stepped into the room. Their first words were: "The Lord is very happy with you. He has bestowed upon you the service of a *Baitul Khayal Kamadia* (the title of one of the custodians for the morning worship)." As I settled in my car outside of our place of worship, I broke down. I cried and cried. I didn't cry because I was worried anymore about the upcoming year. I cried because I considered myself unworthy of the attention that the Lord was bestowing upon me. The year of service that unfolded next was filled with miracles and the presence of the Lord.[145] Later, I realized that the Lord was preparing me for union, a taste of which I would experience a couple of years later at a spiritual gathering.

It was Tuesday morning, April 15, 2008. I was sitting in one

---

[145] In the Relive stage of the "Journey of Presence in God," I describe further the year between July, 2006 and July, 2007.

of the largest halls at the Los Angeles Convention Center with ten thousand other people from our religious community. We were all at the spiritual *Darbar*, meaning the "court of a king" in Farsi. This was the occasion when our spiritual leader and Imam, His Highness the Aga Khan, would visit us and bless us with his physical and spiritual presence, vision and guidance. I was blessed to be one of the three *Waezeen*, faith-based speakers, selected to motivate the members of the community and to prepare them for that occasion in the waiting period.

Finally, my turn came to speak. I remember climbing the stairs and approaching the microphone. This was the largest crowd I had ever served as a faith-based speaker. There was a lot of commotion: many people entering and exiting the halls, small kids crying, older kids bustling with excitement, and many parents and adults wondering how much longer it would be before our spiritual leader arrived. I was used to connecting with a few faces in the audience to personalize my message. However, with the number of people that were there, all I could see were bodies. From my vantage point, they appeared as small as pencils.

I moved to start my presentation and suddenly all went silent. It was as if I was there but no longer there anymore. I could hear myself speaking but it was as if someone else was speaking on my behalf. The presentation was for ten minutes. There was an energy present and active that entire time. I had a script ready on index cards in my hand as to what I was supposed to say; however, I didn't need to reference those notes at any point. The words just flowed as the Lord within me spoke. That moment, the Lord and I were one as his work was to be done. Never before had I experienced such a union in my ability to serve the Lord. I had done many faith-based talks and had always felt inspired from within but this was different. I was witnessing myself speak rather than speaking myself.

As the words came through me, a transformation took over. A lot of people who were entering or exiting stopped where they were and started to listen. I also felt that even though there were thousands of people in the audience, they all felt like one to me. The Lord was speaking and the Lord was listening. As my talk ended, my awareness came back to me. I remembered walking down the stairs of the big stage to sit back down.

How do I explain what occurred that day? The answer may be found in the following words of God spoken through his messenger Muhammad:

> My servant does not approach Me with anything that I love more than the works I have prescribed for him. And he continues to approach Me with supererogatory works until I love him. Then, when I love him, I am his hearing with which he hears, his sight by which he sees, his hand with which he takes hold, his foot with which he walks.[146]

I believe that I experienced this love of the Lord that morning. The Lord was my hearing, seeing, speaking, holding, and walking. I was there merely as a vessel, merely as a witness.

Since that day, before I serve the Lord in any capacity, I whisper in my heart: "Only let those words be said by me that are liked by you, O Lord. Only let those deeds be done by me that are liked by you, O Lord." These are a couple of phrases from devotional poems often recited at our place of worship. They signify the invitation that I extend to the Lord to unify me with his essence and have his will be done, by and through me. I had often imagined that union with God would be like a destination at which I would arrive one day and I would cease to exist and life would be over. On the contrary, my experience has been that it's a journey in which a believer, humble and willing, is taken over by God as God unveils his will, his essence.

Since that April in 2008, I have experienced other such

---

[146] Addas, "Ibn 'Arabi."

moments, sometimes at work, sometimes with family, sometimes during a faith-based talk. Each time, the message has been clear: "ISLAM NOW." As the submission occurs, I witness the Lord take the reins of my life and drive my life where its utility is needed. His light shines, his love extends, his guidance pours, and I'm drenched with a knowing, seeing, and being, like no other. I pray to always rest in this peace, this moment, every moment, this life, every life.

JOURNEY OF UNION WITH GOD
STAGE 6: CONVERSE

My child, I seek unity with you as you seek unity with me.
My life is for you and you alone.

Voices of Man and God

Man: O God, what is your will for our lives?

God: Be kind, be generous, smile often, accept and love others, forgive those that harm you, uplift those that are down, feel the bond that you share with all of humanity, feel your special connection with all of life. Pray not just for yourself but for all others with whom you share life. Serve others for you serve yourself best when you serve them first.

This is what you'll hear every religion tell you. This is what you'll also hear anyone who's vested in a positive society tell you. If one could incorporate this in every citizen of the world, all of world's problems would be gone. I will this for all of life. Truly, I will this first and foremost for myself. Those that are close to my essence reflect each and every one of the above. Since I will this for myself, I will this for the part of me that lives in you, which is the core of you.

Now you may ask, where does union fit into any of this? How come I am not telling you that it's my will that you become one with me?

This is where my will waits. A parent raises his child in the best of ways with the hope that the child will carry forward the work of the parent. Moreover, the parent hopes that the child will always stay near the parent so that the parent can protect the child. But the child, when he/she learns of the world, of the things to do in the world, desires to venture out. The parent sends him out and wishes that the child prosper in every way. It's now up to the child once the child is satisfied from all the worldly explorations and exercise of his/her free will to return to the parent. Thus, when you desire to return to me and

230

submit your will to mine, then the process starts for you to come back home, to be one with me.

The return to me is a very difficult desire to hold. The parent's home is not as attention grabbing as the world. It doesn't have the toys, the entertainment, and the dazzling displays; it does have the feeling of being home and the feeling of being comfortable. You know that feeling when you can be in your pajamas and you know that no one judges you. You can be comfortable in your own skin and everything that you need is always provided. That's the home of your parent.

Man: O God, is it okay for us to love you, to worship you, or to seek you in the form of another human being? What about the form of an object or a symbol?

God: There are those who have worshipped men as Gods. There's nothing wrong in worshiping man as God. Man is, in his essence, God. What's wrong is when a man is worshipped as God exclusively and all of the rest of life is excluded from that Godliness. When this happens, self-righteousness is born as a faithful person only believes in God within a specific being and mistreats all others as unworthy or below God. Nothing is below me, nothing is above me, for everything is in me. As long as you see your focus of love, whether that is Jesus or Krishna or Muhammad, as the stuff that creates and sustains the universe, that lives in all of life, including yourself, then you see and worship God.

There was once a *guru* who was considered by many of his followers to be God. One of his followers was a rational man who found it difficult to see his *guru* as God. One day, the man boldly asked his *guru*: "Dear Master, everyone in the *ashram* considers you to be God. Is it true, are you God?" The *guru* responded: "If your question is coming from a physical perspective, the answer is no. If you consider me God physically, it is as if you worship me like an idol without an essence. Now, if your question is whether I am God from a spiritual perspective, in that case, my son, within the context of spirituality, the question doesn't arise. Because in the spiritual realm, not only am I God, but you, too, are God; in fact all of life is God."

I believe this is the best answer for your question. When you observe someone worshipping another human being as God, from your remote point of view, you only see the form, you don't see the essence; you don't see what's in the heart of the one worshipping. Without this knowledge, it's impossible to judge whether or not such worship is right or wrong. Sometimes, even the one worshipping doesn't truly know the depth of his/her own faith. This knowledge only resides with me. It's best, then, to not judge, to let everyone have their own faith, to let everyone practice their way of connecting with me. Learn from all and find the way that suits you best, that brings you closest to me.

What I have discussed above about a human being equally applies to symbols or objects.

Man: O God, you said earlier that it's our will that initiates the process of union with your essence. You also said that this union can occur through any medium of our choosing: a human or a symbol or an object. But why should we strive for this union? Until now, I don't feel I have heard a clear case for prioritizing this aspect of life more than any other. Especially if we have access to your presence, why strive for union?

God: What if I gave you a trick present in which there are multiple boxes to open before you get to the innermost box which contains a beautiful treasure? You won't be satisfied until you reach the core because until you do, all you'll have is a box. A box is not a gift, it's just a shell. Striving for union is the same way. It's looking for the inner most treasure. In some ways, the word "union" is a misnomer for that assumes that there are two items that are meeting together. Rather, there's only one item at the core and the rest of it needs to be sifted through to arrive at that core, at that one item. Most of you live life at the level of a box. Some have penetrated deeper than others but even those who have penetrated deeper are still not at the innermost core. Sure, you have the presence of the core like I described in the earlier journey but that lasts a few moments. What's experienced in union is much longer, much deeper, much more at the core level than anything else.

Now this won't interest someone who doesn't understand that life is like a trick box. For he/she will judge himself/herself as one of the boxes and will decorate that box with worldly identifications to make that box visible and valuable in the eyes of all others. But eventually, all of those decorations will wither as the individual comes closer and closer to his physical demise or experiences some tragedy. Then the individual wonders: "Is this truly all I am, a bag of bones with some thoughts and feelings? Is there nothing more to my existence?" Usually, by the time these thoughts initiate, the individual is already at the lower rungs of physical life and soon time runs out and the journey must continue for a later time.

My desire for you is that you desire to return home, to find the inner box, sooner rather than later. The sooner you desire this, the sooner you'll seek out the divine not just within yourself but in all of life. You'll see God as beyond the form of your desire, the symbol, the idol, the human being. You'll see God within and without. The Kingdom of God will be everywhere and as you go deeper and deeper in that kingdom, you'll identify your connection with all others in this life. You'll feel oneness, integrity, and love at the core. The closer you get to the core, the more you will emanate the qualities of the core. Accordingly, the more goodness and Godliness will come through you into your life and the lives of all others. Eventually, the goal of your highest desire, the union, or better yet, the extinction in me will be reached. The innermost box will be revealed and the treasure of love and light will be found.

Man: O God, what's the best way to seek union with you?

God: I have provided many ladders to reach me. For many, the ladders are the teachers and the messengers who have walked amongst you and whose love and light you carry in your hearts. For others, it's the Holy Spirit, which is nothing more than my breath, my light, which forms the core identity or spirit of each human being. Each religion is a ladder to reach me, a way towards the peak of the mountain, which leads to God. I have provided the means for all to return back to their original home, to be one with me.

It doesn't matter which means you choose as long as you choose with faith and you practice with sincerity. When you give yourself to the practice of oneness, oneness penetrates your being. One way as we discussed earlier is to find a word that reminds you of God. This word needs to be special to you, special in that you believe that it's a key to get you to God. Your belief in this word and your practice of it in moments of quiet and solitude, what's also referred to as meditation, will bring you closer and closer to my Light. This is the simplest way of becoming one with my presence.

But guard well your thoughts, words, deeds, and especially feelings throughout each day. Don't let your mind, body, and soul be taken over by negative thoughts and emotions. Such thoughts and emotions act negatively not only on the body, as science has already proven, but also on the soul. They take you away from me. They create noise so that you are unable to see my presence, to feel union, to experience the destruction of the shells or identities, the boxes that we identified earlier.

When you finally reach me, you become a piece of my peace. You become an extension of my being. You become the flame of my light. You become a form of me. It's a powerful way to exist. It's a powerful means to bring change into all of life. It's growth and love at its utmost. Some have called this the brotherhood of light. Some have called this the emissaries of peace. Whatever name you call it with, what it is, is good and what it is, is God.

I grow in you and you grow in me. We partner to live life together to bring about my will on earth and beyond. Presence can prepare one for such an experience. But presence is more about acquiring peace in one's life so that one can pursue union. Union is the ultimate journey of all of life and once achieved, there's nothing more to journey towards.

JOURNEY OF UNION WITH GOD
STAGE 7: REALIZE

I now swim the ocean of my life
with clear union with God.
I live my life as his life
bringing peace to all I encounter.

Voice of Reader

As I return back to my day to day life, I reflect on the following questions to apply lessons from this journey:
- What new insights did I receive through this journey about life and about God?

- What changes will I make in my daily life as a result of these new insights?

- How will these changes help me live a more fulfilled and meaningful life?

GOD'S WORD

Dear Reader, I am so happy that you have come to the end of the seven journeys to be one with God. If you have truly given yourself to these journeys, I have no doubt that you feel me now pulsating in your being and living. Even as you read these words, you can feel a part of you that recognizes the writing on this page. I am that old friend, who has been with you through every moment of your life: through every challenge, every difficulty, every joy, and every celebration. I am truly the only complete companion that you can ever have in life for I am eternal and my company is eternal.

Before this book ends, I want to address a few questions that you may have about this book. First, why did I choose to have this book manifest in your experience of life? After all, there's no shortage of books from and about God. Why provide an additional message to humanity from and about God and why in this format?

Before humanity came into being, I created a light from my light that would exist to guide and sustain all of life through age and time. This light was perfect intelligence, perfect beauty, perfect grace, and perfect love. This light had the capacity to create and sustain universes. It's with this light that I created mankind and it's this light that lives in the heart of each human being as the essence of my being. It's through this light that all messages to humanity have come to mankind. Since this light resides in each human being, it's usually a human being who's close to this light who reveals the message to the rest. In this way, many teachers have come forth, many messages have been brought forward, and many religions have been born.

But in this process, it was never my intention for you to use these messages to divide yourselves into different religious or spiritual groups and consider yourselves better or more guided or closer to me than your fellow brothers and sisters in life. Rather, I intended for you to see the unity in all of the messages and all of the messengers. That way you would know the unity in all of life, and the light behind it all. This is the same light that resides in each and every one of you. Having known the light, you would strive together to be one with that light and to live from that light.

Somehow, this got lost in your interpretation of the messages and the lives of the messengers. The book that you have completed strives to correct this. It strives to help you realize that the teachers, some of whom are considered the founders of different religions, were inspired by the same source. They all carried the same message that it was mankind's purpose to return to their source, to be one with God, through finding their inner being, the inner light in their own hearts.

To deliver this teaching, this book has been organized in a format of seven journeys. As you may have observed, in their essence, each of these seven journeys is exactly the same. It's just that they approach oneness with God from a different perspective. I am aware that each of you has a different approach to God. So for each, at least one journey was made available through which he/she can become one with God. In the end, all seven journeys lead to the same place, the same state, the same goal: I am that goal.

Another question that you may have is about the author of this book, Shafeen Ali. Why is this teaching coming through him rather than anyone else? Shafeen has asked me this question himself many times. He has always had a very personal relationship with me, seeing me present in every aspect of his life. It has taken immense courage on his part to make his personal relationship public through this book. But he, too, has wondered why he was asked to do this work by his Inner Imam? I have only one answer for him and for you. He's my "spiritual son."

There are only a few people in the world today that truly consider themselves to be my children. Fewer still, have a relationship with me where they can talk to me directly. Through this book, I envision a world in which more and more spiritual children will be encouraged to communicate with me directly, to find my love and light within their being and be available to bring that love and light into the world.

The last question that I would like to address is the following: Will there be other messages after this book, other ways for me to help you get in touch with the essence of my love and light within your being? The answer is "YES!" This book will give the courage to many of my spiritual children to a) speak to me directly and b) make my message to humanity heard. I'll certainly continue to work through Shafeen to provide to you my guidance. But I want you to know that the objective of this book is not for you to solely depend on someone or something external, any one person or symbol or group or book, to be one with God. Everything and everyone external is a reminder for the one within, for my essence within. The objective is for each and every one of you to find the way to me within, to your personal connection with me in your heart, to your living and breathing of me in your life.

This doesn't mean that you have to leave your religious or spiritual community to find me. Rather, this means that you have to engage deeper in your religious or spiritual community through those practices that develop your personal connection with me and thus with your own inner being. I am waiting for you to call out to me in such ways so that I can enlighten your life, both physically and spiritually, both temporally and eternally.

Each of you has your own light, your own direct connection to me. Enliven that connection and talk to me today, this moment, and every moment. I am available to you as I am available to each and every one of my spiritual sons and daughters. I love each and every one of you equally. It's up to you though to make that love and light a part of your life. So begin today, begin now. Don't let this book and its message ever end. Embrace me this moment and I promise you that you'll never lose me again. Even if you fall in darkness, I'll bring you back to my light.

It's now time for me to end and for you to begin. There's

nothing more to be said except this: I am waiting for you, my child. Re-member me, I will re-member you!

Eternally yours,

Your Beloved Spiritual Father!

BIBLIOGRAPHY

Addas, Claude. "The experience and doctrine of love in Ibn 'Arabi." The Muhyiddin Ibn 'Arabi Society. Translated by Cecilia Twinch. Accessed August 18, 2015. http://www.ibnarabisociety.org/articles/addas1.html.

Albom, Mitch. *Have a Little Faith: A True Story*. New York, NY: Hyperion Books, 2009.

Arberry, A. J., trans. *Muslim Saints and Mystics*. Ames, IA: Omphaloskepsis, 2000.

Aslan, Reza. *No God But God: The Origins, Evolution, and Future of Islam*. London, UK: Arrow Books, 2006.

Attar, Farid Ud-Din, *The Conference of the Birds*. Translated by Afkham Darbandi and Dick Davis. London, UK: Penguin Books, 1984.

Chidvilasananda, Gurumayi. *Kindle My Heart: A Collection Of Talks by Gurumayi Chidvilasananda*. South Fallsburg, NY: SYDA Foundation, 1989.

Cooper, John M., and D. S. Hutchinson, eds. *Plato Complete Works*. Indianapolis, IN: Hackett Publishing Company, 1997.

De Mello, S. J., Anthony. *The Song of the Bird*. 2nd ed. Anand, India: Gujarat Sahitya Prakash, 1982.

Easwaran, Eknath, trans. *The Bhagavad Gita*. 2nd ed. Tomales, CA: Nilgiri Press, 2007.

Fadiman, James, and Robert Frager, eds. *Essential Sufism*. Edison, NJ: Castle Books, 1998.

Furey, Robert J. *The Joy of Kindness*. Chestnut Ridge, NY: Crossroad Publishing Company, 1993.

Jammer, Max. *Einstein and Religion: Physics and Theology*. Princeton, NJ: Princeton University Press, 1999.

Johnson, Caesar. *To See a World in a Grain of Sand*. Norwalk, CN: C.R. Gibson Co., 1972.

Kohn, Sherab. *A Life of the Buddha*. Rev. ed. Boston, MA: Shambhala Publications, 2009.

Lutgendorf, Philip. *Hanuman's Tale: The Messages of a Divine Monkey*. New York, NY: Oxford University Press, 2007.

McTaggart, Lynne. *The Field: The Quest for the Secret Force of the Universe*. New York, NY: HarperCollins Publishers, 2002.

Mitchell, Robert A. *The Buddha: His Life Retold*. New York, NY: Paragon House, 1989.

Rumi, Jalalu-'d-din. *The Masnavi I Ma'navi of Rumi*. Translated by Edward Whinfield. London, UK: Forgotten Books, 2008.

Vanamali. *The Complete Life of Krishna: Based on the Earliest Oral Traditions and the Sacred Scriptures*. Rep. ed. Rochester, VT: Inner Traditions, 2012. EPUB e-Book.
————. *The Complete Life of Rama: Based on Valmiki's Ramayana and the Earliest Oral Traditions*. Rep. ed. Rochester, VT: Inner Traditions, 2014.

ABOUT THE AUTHOR

Shafeen Ali is a Shia Ismaili Muslim who has been a faith-based teacher and speaker for the last 10 years. He has delivered more than 150 presentations and workshops throughout the world on faith and religious education. Shafeen also has a Masters in Business Administration and has spent more than 13 years managing and executing business and technology projects and teams in the United States.

The source of strength and guidance in Shafeen's life has always been the spirit of God within, his Inner Imam. Through this book, Shafeen is externalizing that innermost part of him with the hope and prayer that this spirit will provide strength and guidance to others just as it has done for him.

Shafeen currently resides with his family in Euless, Texas. To contact him, please visit his website: www.ShafeenAli.com.

Made in the USA
Middletown, DE
31 January 2016